LEBEK

Although Lebek is a fictional city, its Bronze Age megaliths, medieval guildhalls, and bustling seventeenth-century port mirror developments in actual cities of Picardy (France), Flanders (Belgium), the German regions of Frisia, Lower Saxony, Mecklenburg, Pomerania, and East Prussia, as well as in the Netherlands. Lebek's "history" is a compilation of the political, economic, and social histories of those cities. Its "evolution" reflects events and institutions that combined to form such vibrant Northern European urban centers as Rotterdam, Hamburg, Amsterdam, Kiel, Lübeck, Rostock, and Danzig.

Whatever their differences, these ports of the Baltic and North seas shared three formative influences: the sea, an entrepreneurial spirit, and a morality shaped by the severe tenets of the Protestant Reformation. In their earliest phases their remoteness from the Greco-Roman culture flourishing to the south allowed them to develop independently. During the Middle Ages, the sea offered them a route to political and economic autonomy within the feudal system. Later, it drew many of these same cities together under the banner of the Hanseatic League, the maritime trade alliance that established them as formidable and enormously prosperous links in European routes to the East Indies and the New World. Today, the sea, commerce, banking, commercial fisheries, manufacturing, and industry remain their common fundamental components.

Lebek's "history" is, in a certain sense, a condensation of the history of coastal Northern Europe. The large illustrations and main text offer casual browsers a clear overview. Readers seeking greater elaboration will find it in sidebars and detailed drawings. Those wishing to go still further will find ample material here for provocative discussion, heated debate, or quiet reflection on the subject of why cities arise and how they persist.

Printed in Italy

10 9 8 7 6 5 4 3 2 1

Library of Congress Cataloging-in-Publication Data

Hernandez, Xavier.
    Lebek : a hanseatic city of Northern Europe / Xavier Hernandez,
Jordi Ballonga ; illustrated by Francesco Corni; translated by
Kathleen Leverich.
    p. cm.
    Reprint. Originally published: Italy : Editoriale Jaca Book SpA,
1991.
    ISBN 0-395-57442-0
    1. Hansa towns—History. 2. Cities and towns—Europe, Northern—
History. 3. Coasts—Europe, Northern—History. I. Comes, Pilar.
II. Ballonga, Jordi. III. Title.
DD801.H21H47 1991
943.1'5'009732—dc20   90-22191
                                                                 CIP

LEBEK

A CITY
OF NORTHERN EUROPE
THROUGH THE AGES

XAVIER HERNÁNDEZ · JORDI BALLONGA

Illustrated by
FRANCESCO CORNI

Translated by Kathleen Leverich

Houghton Mifflin Company
Boston 1991

1. SETTLEMENTS AND STANDING STONES: 1000 B.C.

1. Settlements and Standing Stones

1000 B.C.

Around the tenth century B.C., Bronze Age peoples established themselves in the lowlands of Northern Europe. Some built settlements on the gentle hills that ringed the estuary of a large river, known even then as the Leb. Fierce northwest winds and storms periodically sent the sea pouring over the lowlands, flooding all in its path. On the partly secure hillsides, the new settlers practiced a precarious form of agriculture. The interior provided grazing lands for flocks. Fishing and the harvesting of shellfish in the Leb estuary soon became important components of the subsistence economy of the region. Gradually, the people developed an understanding of the seasonal weather patterns and their effect on the marshes, dunes, and tidal flood plain. As understanding increased, fear of the estuary and the powerful forces of nature that

1. Ceremonial Site
Megalithic monuments served a variety of purposes. Some were religious sites, others tombs. Some complexes appear to have been designed as mammoth calendars, in which the stones acted as reference points to observe stars and mark seasons.

2. Settlements
The ancients built their settlements on the hillsides, out of the reach of flood tides and storms that periodically submerged the lowlands. They used reclaimed lands on the village outskirts for farming.

3. Coastal Shoals and Bars
Materials eroded from coastal reefs, as well as silt and debris carried downstream by the river, formed deposits at the estuary's entrance. These deposits created shoals and fingerlike bars that pointed the direction of coastal currents.

4. Dunes
Wind buffeted the coastal sands that were exposed at low tide, to create dunes. These continued to shift until natural or cultivated vegetation grew over their surfaces and anchored them in place. In some cases an accumulation of dunes served to block an estuary entrance, forming a lagoon.

5. Marshes
Buffering shoals and dunes created stretches of stagnant water along the mainland. Mud and silt carried downstream by the river contributed to the formation of marshes. As silt accumulated, salt-tolerant vegetation sprang up. Gradually, the land stabilized and dried out. It was suitable for tilling, but remained dangerously prone to floods.

Stone Quarrying
To extract slabs of the desired dimensions from the quarry, stonemasons equipped with quartz hammers cut deep mortises, or cavities, into the solid stone. They drove wooden wedges into the mortises, and soaked the wedges with water. The moistened wedges expanded and eventually split the rock along the desired lines.

converged there decreased.

Peoples throughout Northern Europe were creating ceremonial sites composed of tall stone slabs, or megaliths. Several Leb settlements united to build a sanctuary of standing stones upon a firm stretch of land close to the sea. The work lasted for years, with laborers numbering in the hundreds. Both men and women joined in the work of wresting huge slabs from remote inland cliffs and dragging them laboriously to the coastal site. Masons skilled in the use of stone picks and bronze tools hewed the megaliths and supervised their placement.

The sanctuary consisted of long rows of standing stones. The site also served as a solar calendar. By observing the changing positions of the stones' shadows, the people could track the planting and harvesting sea-

sons and anticipate periods of storms, northwest winds, and abundant fish.

The coastal lands surrounding the Leb remained sparsely populated for hundreds of years. Only at the beginning of the Christian era did Germanic tribes migrate to the region and establish themselves on the sites of the ancient settlements. In the intervening centuries the landscape had subtly changed. Burial mounds and debris of all kinds acted as landfill to increase the size of the hills. At the same time, other lands were lost to the sea. The new inhabitants labored to reclaim those submerged lands. With great difficulty, they erected breakwaters and dikes of mud and straw. The parcels regained were added to the acreage of tillable fields. Thus began the titanic struggle for land between the people of the Leb region and the sea.

Raising a Standing Stone
Workers dug a deep hole. The stone slab was dragged up an embankment to the hole's edge. Laborers using ropes and levers rolled the great stone into the hole, where it landed and remained upright.

Transporting Megaliths
The massive stones could weigh as much as forty tons, but they were moved great distances by means of timber rollways. Two hundred or more people dragged each stone, which moved slowly forward over these timber conveyors. The timbers at the rear were carried forward to extend the rollway farther.

2. "DRAGONS" FROM THE NORTH: Late Eighth Century A.D.

2. "Dragons" from the North

Late Eighth Century A.D.

As the centuries passed, the Leb estuary underwent successive physical transformations. The clearing and cultivation of inland areas caused an increase in the amount of silt carried and deposited in the estuary.

Meanwhile, the Germanic peoples who lived along the northern coast and the Leb remained unaffected by Roman civilization to the south. They continued their ancestral forms of life, disturbed only by occasional migrations of peoples from the west.

At the beginning of the eighth century A.D. the pace of life along the Leb estuary suddenly quickened. New settlers arrived in large numbers and began rapidly to form a city on one of the river isles. In contrast to earlier migrants, these new inhabitants came not from the west or the interior, but from beyond the northern seas.

Viking fleets had for decades paid sporadic and destructive visits to the Leb estuary. The Norsemen came to loot and pillage, but also to search for lands to colonize. Their own lands could not provide adequate

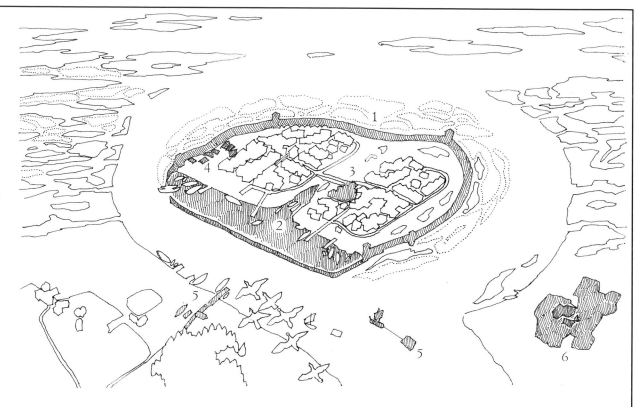

1. Defensive Walls
Embankments reinforced with wooden palisades protected the city from possible surprise attacks. Wooden barricades also protected the port.

2. Port
The port was sited out of the way of strong river currents. The Vikings' light-hulled ships could be beached rather than left at anchor, for greater security. Ships from the most remote regions of the North and Baltic seas visited the harbor. Their cargoes were stored in nearby warehouses.

3. Residential Districts
The city's merchants, artisans, and mariners occupied modest, thatched-roof houses of mud, straw, and brambles. To create firm roadbeds on the boggy earth, some streets were paved with wooden planking.

4. Traders' Encampment
Traders lodged in huts or tents that were easily dismantled.

5. Shipyards
The Vikings were skilled shipbuilders, and the forests of the interior provided an abundance of timber. Once shipped downriver, this timber was unloaded in well organized and equipped shipyards. There, it was fashioned into ocean-going ships and river vessels.

6. Farm
The Vikings cultivated fields and kept sheep and cows. Granaries, stables, storehouses, and slave quarters were all grouped around the central residence.

Viking House
① Mortarless stone walls, reinforced with timbering.
② Thatched roof.
③ Hearth.
④ Loom.
⑤ Beds.

food to support a growing population.

The sheltered Leb estuary presented an appealing refuge to the Vikings. They chose an easily defensible river isle as the site of their settlement and the anchorage for their fleet. This island base offered them rapid access both to open sea and to upriver refuges. *Drakkars*, the swift Viking ships, ranged over coastal and river waters, staging surprise attacks on any settlements they discovered. The distinctive dragon-head-shaped prow advancing over the waters struck terror in the hearts of all who saw it.

As time passed, the Viking encampment developed into a stable city and assumed the name Levfjord. Looting and pillage gradually gave way to an enterprise that proved more lucrative and less risky: commerce.

Levfjord, governed by the Viking nobility, became a prosperous market town. Ships from northern seas and barges from the interior, motivated by a shared eagerness to trade, met at its wharves. Salt fish, slaves, leather goods, woolens, pottery, iron and bronze cookware, amber beads, tools, weapons, and rope were all auctioned to the highest bidders.

Levfjord prospered. New fields on its outskirts were cleared and planted. Its craftsmen produced firearms and fine woolen cloth. As the Vikings intermarried with the indigenous peoples and adopted the Christian faith, the wars of earlier periods ended. At the beginning of the eleventh century, Levfjord, commonly known by the name Lebeckburg, although absorbed into the feudal fiefdom of the Lower Leb, managed to retain its autonomy.

① Hull.
② Planking.
③ Beams.
④ Mast step.
⑤ Prow, being sculpted into the shape of a dragon's head.
⑥ Starboard rudder.

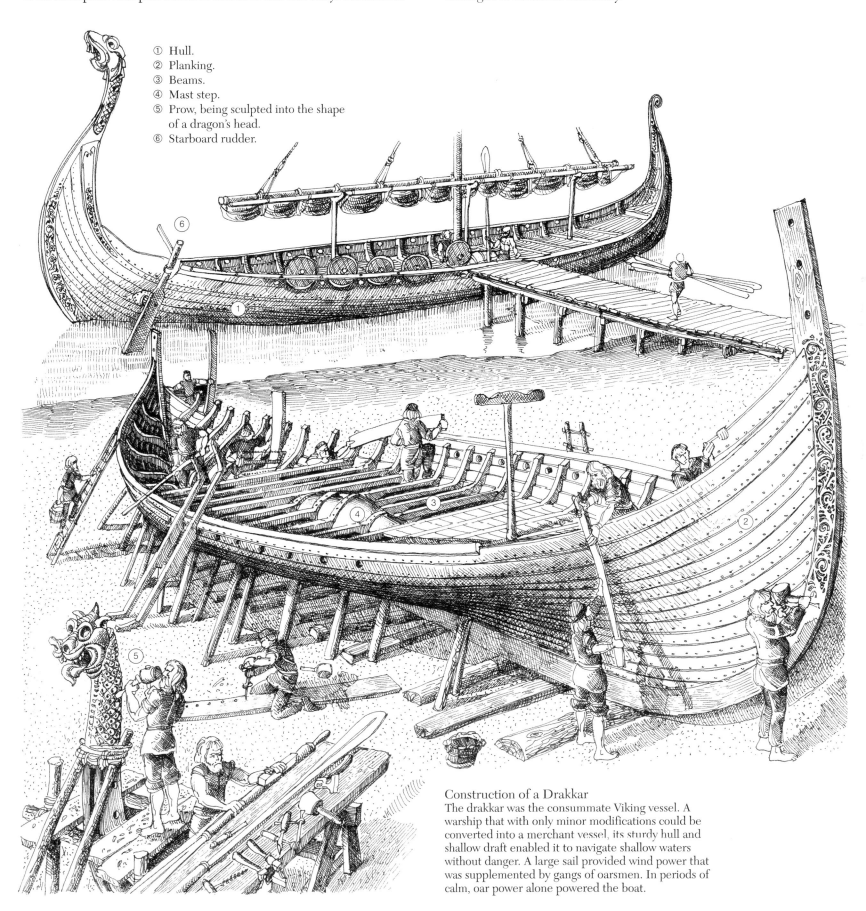

Construction of a Drakkar
The drakkar was the consummate Viking vessel. A warship that with only minor modifications could be converted into a merchant vessel, its sturdy hull and shallow draft enabled it to navigate shallow waters without danger. A large sail provided wind power that was supplemented by gangs of oarsmen. In periods of calm, oar power alone powered the boat.

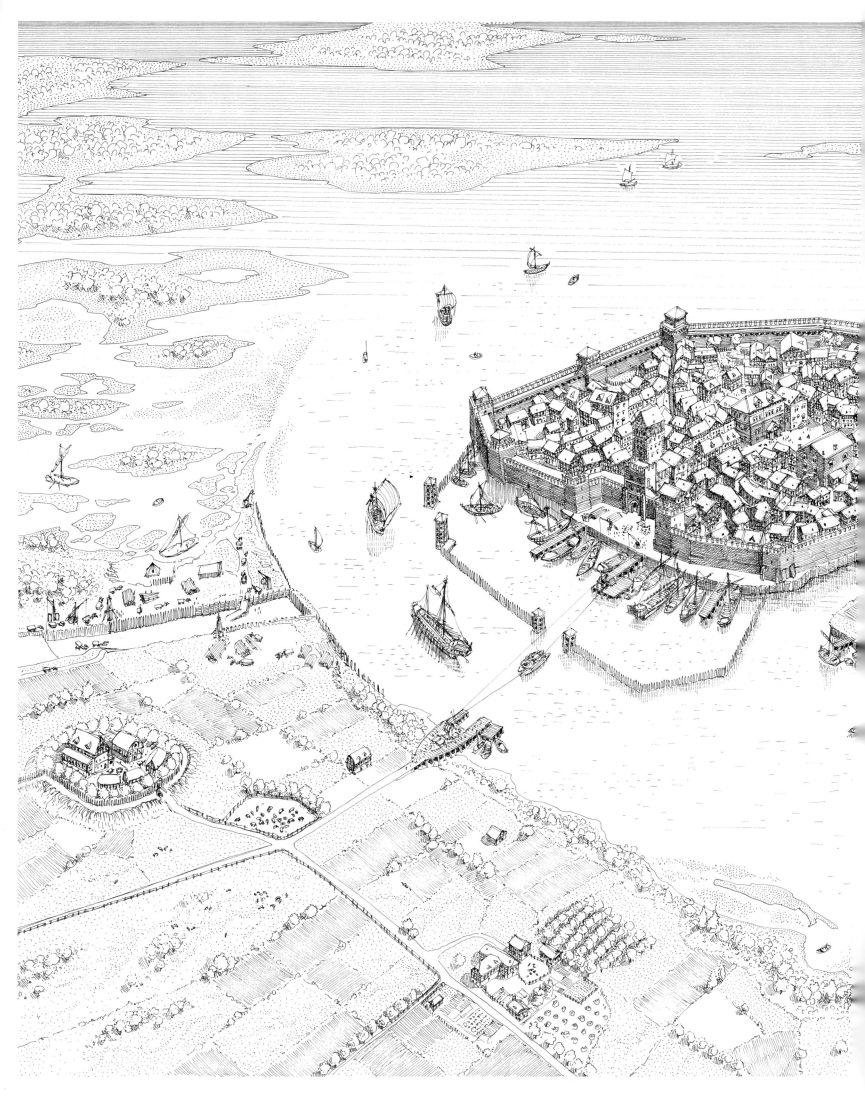

3. FREE CITY IN FEUDAL EUROPE: Early Thirteenth Century

3. Free City in Feudal Europe
Early Thirteenth Century

By the end of the twelfth century, trade along the southern coasts of the North and Baltic seas was undergoing major transformations. The flow of commerce had formerly been based on the haphazard comings and goings of traders and a simple barter economy. Now, commercial transactions were promoted and their volume and frequency increased through the introduction of formal accounting procedures, the extension of credit, and the payment of commissions to merchant middlemen. The Viking drakkars of the past were replaced by *koggen*, new vessels that weighed up to one hundred tons. At the same time, the merchants of the ports of the North and Baltic seas united to better defend their interests. One particular group formed a trade cooperative known as the Hanse. The merchants of the Leb estuary joined them.

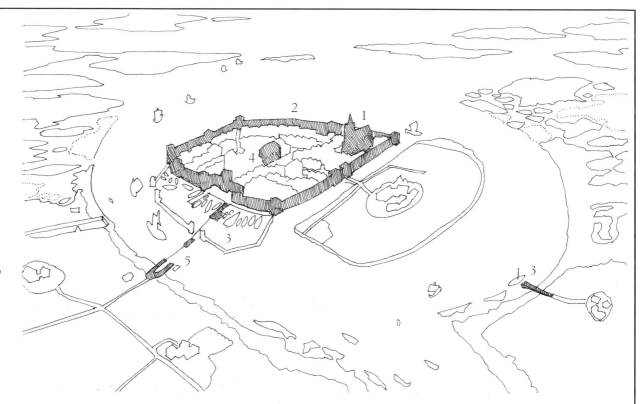

1. Romanesque Cathedral
This church was built of stone slabs, in the distinctive style originating in France and Germany. Its solid structure contrasted sharply with the city's flimsy dwellings. As was common practice during the medieval period, the cathedral's construction was financed by contributions from artisans' and merchants' guilds.

2. City Walls
The walls were built of stone and mortar, reinforced with timber. They protected the population from surprise attacks by sea or land. Unfortunately the walls also created an obstacle to communication between the wharves and the city proper.

3. Wharves
At the beginning of the thirteenth century, most ships in common use still weighed relatively little and could be beached on the mainland's sands. The larger, weightier ships floated at moorings in the shelter of mainland stockades, to which they were connected by wooden gangways.

4. Diet
The Diet, or council, met in a centrally located hall. Documents and archives were stored there.

5. Ferries
Cable-driven barges linked Lebek to the mainland.

Construction Phases of a Typical House
① The wooden frame and crossbeams were built of timber brought from the nearest forest.
② Walls were framed, woven with brambles, and plastered. In later times brick walls would come into common use.
③ The framed roof was covered with thatch.

Lebeckburg, now known as Lebek, had long forgotten its Viking origins. The pirates and Scandinavian warriors whose ships occasionally appeared in the Leb estuary were regarded as dangerous savages. Lebek's allegiances and interests all bound it firmly to its continental neighbors. As a port and a member of the Hanseatic League, the city realized substantial benefits from the opening of new commercial routes on the North and Baltic seas.

Although the city was technically a fief of the Lower Leb's feudal duchy, Lebek maintained a broad measure of political autonomy and was exempted from many of the duties and taxes commonly levied. The feudal lord extended these privileges to Lebek's citizens, in exchange for the city's nominal pledge of fealty. Lebek's evolving maritime trade ben-

efited the entire fiefdom, enabling it to develop a self-sufficient, farm-based economy. The produce of the fields, the wool of the flocks, and the cloth produced by the Leb area peasants, all found buyers in this thriving mercantile port.

Although some members of the nobility participated in the city's commercial life, Lebek's principal merchants were its primary managers and directors. The Diet, or city council, was enpowered to regulate daily life within the city, while solid encircling walls of stone and timber protected it from land and sea attacks. A Romanesque cathedral occupied a prominent position within those walls, which likewise sheltered the dwellings of artisans, merchants, and mariners. A central square, where the Diet hall was situated, formed one of the few open spaces.

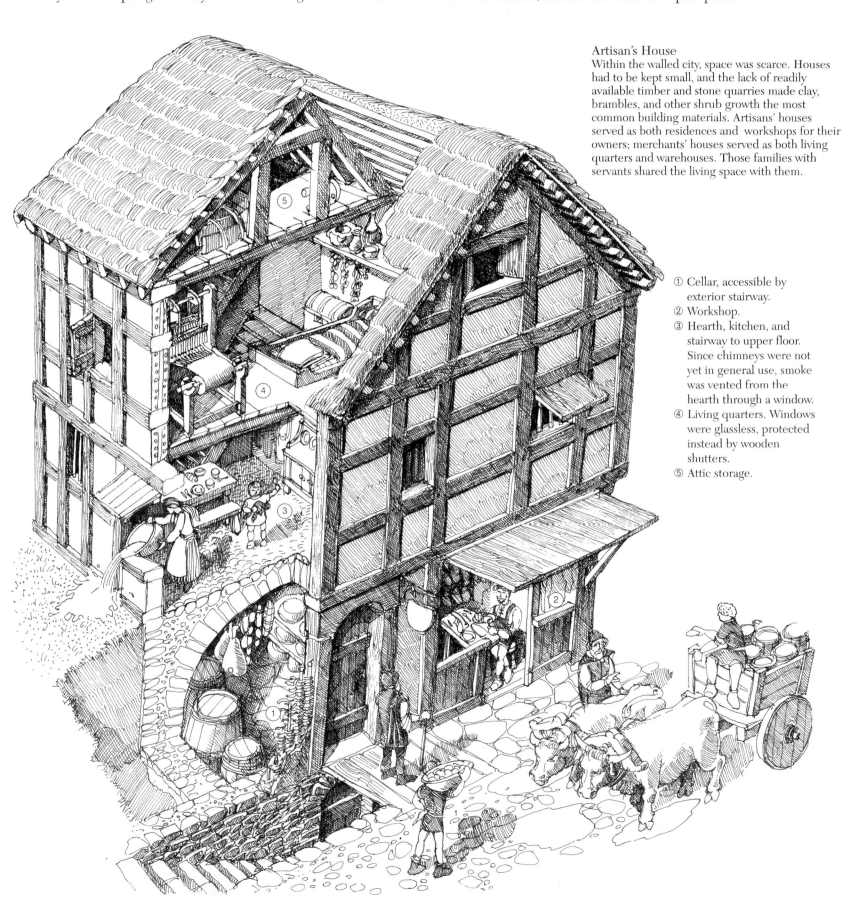

Artisan's House
Within the walled city, space was scarce. Houses had to be kept small, and the lack of readily available timber and stone quarries made clay, brambles, and other shrub growth the most common building materials. Artisans' houses served as both residences and workshops for their owners; merchants' houses served as both living quarters and warehouses. Those families with servants shared the living space with them.

① Cellar, accessible by exterior stairway.
② Workshop.
③ Hearth, kitchen, and stairway to upper floor. Since chimneys were not yet in general use, smoke was vented from the hearth through a window.
④ Living quarters. Windows were glassless, protected instead by wooden shutters.
⑤ Attic storage.

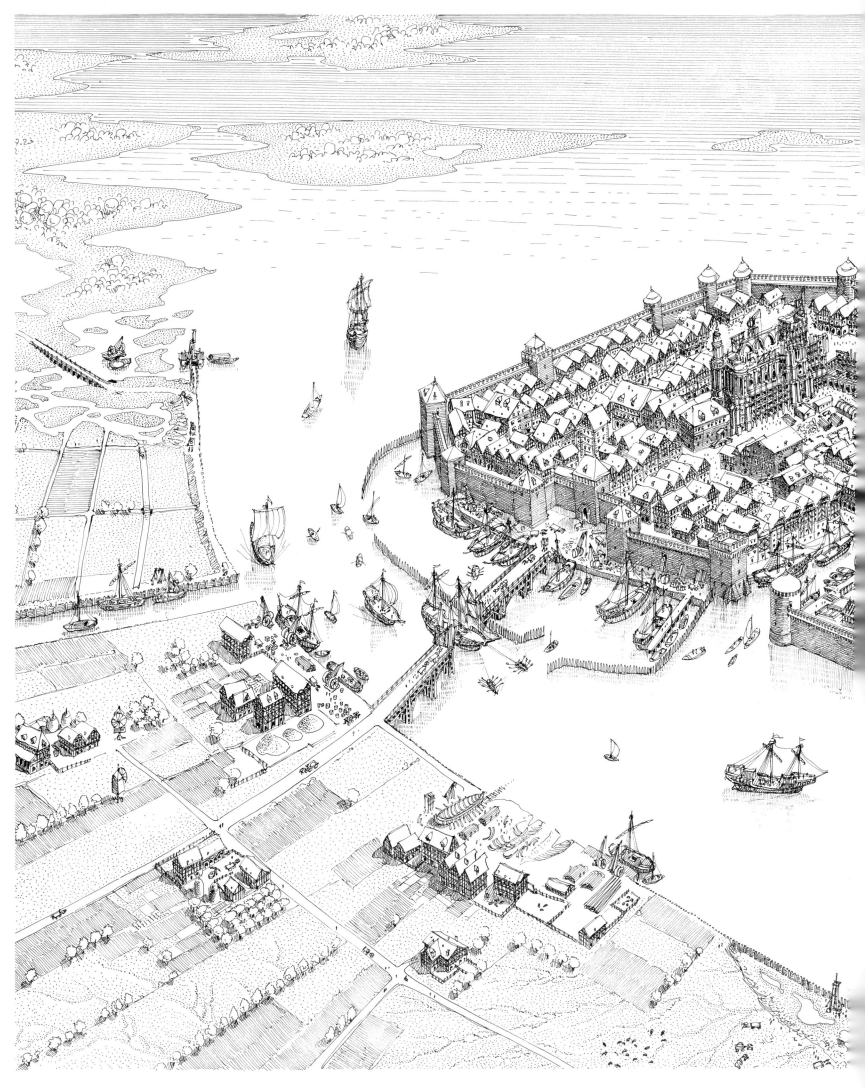

4. THE CITY BUILT UPON HERRING: Mid-Fourteenth Century

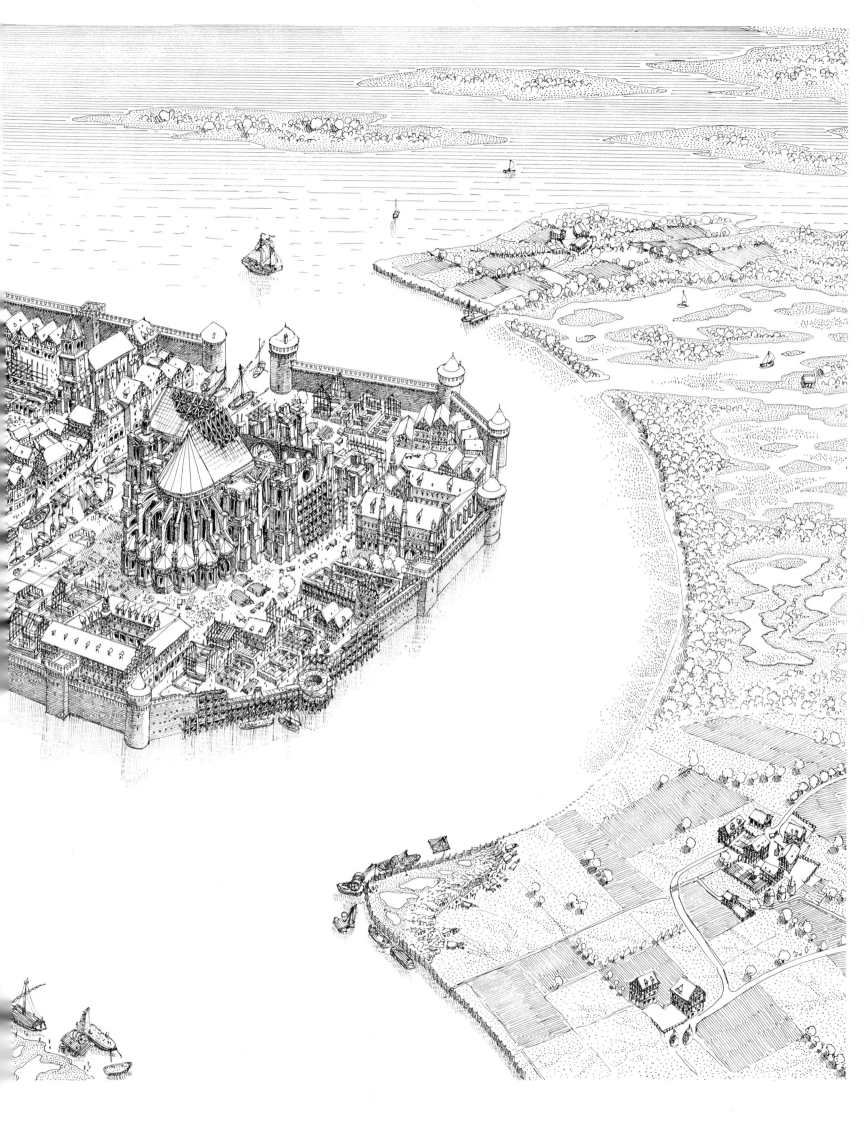

4. The City Built upon Herring
Mid-Fourteenth Century

During the late Middle Ages, Lebek continued to prosper and expand through trade. While its site on the Germanic coast made membership in the Hanseatic League a logical necessity, Lebek's sphere of influence extended far beyond. Merchants cultivated close ties with a similar confederation in Flanders, and with trading partners in Picardy and Britain.

Ships of every description and nationality visited Lebek's wharves. Vessels from the distant Mediterranean ports of Genoa, Marseilles, and Catalonia arrived carrying cargoes of spices, alum, silk, glass, and wine. Ships from the French Atlantic came laden with salt. From the Baltic arrived vessels loaded with hides, iron, copper, and smoked fish.

Lebek had its own goods to offer in exchange. Fine woolen cloth was available from the city's own workshops, as well as from inland regions

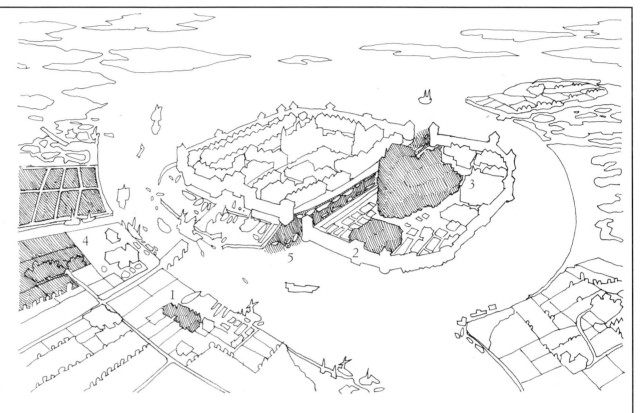

1. Herring Processing Plant
Fishing fleets caught enormous quantities of herring. Fish were gutted and conveyed to a processing plant where they were salted and packed into wooden barrels. Smoke processing was less widely practiced, as was drying, a process applied only to cod.

2. Hospital
Hospitals were built to care for the sick and injured, and to improve the overall quality of city life. Typically, these medical centers were established and run by members of religious orders. Physicians of the era drew on empirical knowledge, folk wisdom, and superstition in their efforts to cure the sick.

3. Cathedral
The great Gothic cathedrals that rose in the cities of Northern Europe took as their models those being built farther south. Soaring vertical lines characterized these structures, as did elaborate exteriors. Construction was slow and commonly employed several generations of stonemasons and architects. Each new generation brought to the original plan improved techniques and design modifications.

4. Farms
The struggle to reclaim land from the sea continued on the outskirts of the city. The work was long and hard, and the returns small. Dikes had to be raised, and the lands drained and desalinated. As each new parcel was reclaimed for cultivation, a farm sprang up on it. One storm tide or one seasonal flood, however, was enough to wipe out all fruits of these enormous labors.

5. Canal
Lowland cities often used interior canals as substitutes for streets. Canals offered easy access to the city center and provided an outlet for flood waters. Transport canals were often dug in inland areas to connect rivers and other canals. The river transport system these created provided faster, more economical transport than land routes.

Cathedral Construction Phases
① Land was graded and the cathedral foundation excavated.
② Walls, pilasters, columns, and apse buttresses were erected.
③ The roof was raised, and the transept built.

①

②

of the Upper Leb. In addition to cloth, a multitude of other products moved downriver to the city: weapons, iron, and livestock.

Lebek possessed one resource whose importance dwarfed all others: salt herring. The city maintained a large fishing fleet that worked the rich herring banks in the shallows off its coast. Catches were taken to processing plants where they were salted and packed into barrels. Once processed, the fish could be kept and eaten for up to a year. Lebek's plants exported thousands of barrels to cities all over Europe, above all to the cities of the Mediterranean. Rich in protein, inexpensive, and easily kept, salt herring saved many of medieval Europe's urban lower classes from hunger and malnutrition. For Lebek, herring served as the gold that financed expansion.

The isle in the Leb consisted of two sections: the walled city and a largely unsettled tract. The broad canal that separated the two provided easy access to ships with cargoes to load and unload. As Lebek's popula-tion grew, the city expanded into the open space on the canal's far side. In this new district, a hospital was built by a religious order. The city fathers began other ambitious urban development projects, including the construction of a great Gothic cathedral. Merchants' and artisans' guilds joined with the Church in financing and erecting this structure, whose brilliance of design and engineering equaled those rising in Northern Europe's other major urban centers.

Redevelopment projects in Lebek's main market square included con-struction of an impressive new Diet, emblematic of the free city's growing wealth and power. Construction also began on privately held buildings, as Lebek's most important commercial entities vied to outdo one another in the creation of palatial headquarters. In residential districts, old dwellings were demolished to make way for larger, comfortable houses. Lebek was in full flower.

Northern European Gothic Cathedral
① Façade and spires.
② Buttresses and flying buttresses.
③ Nave.
④ Aisles.
⑤ Entrance.
⑥ Apse.
⑦ Stained glass windows.
⑧ Plan.

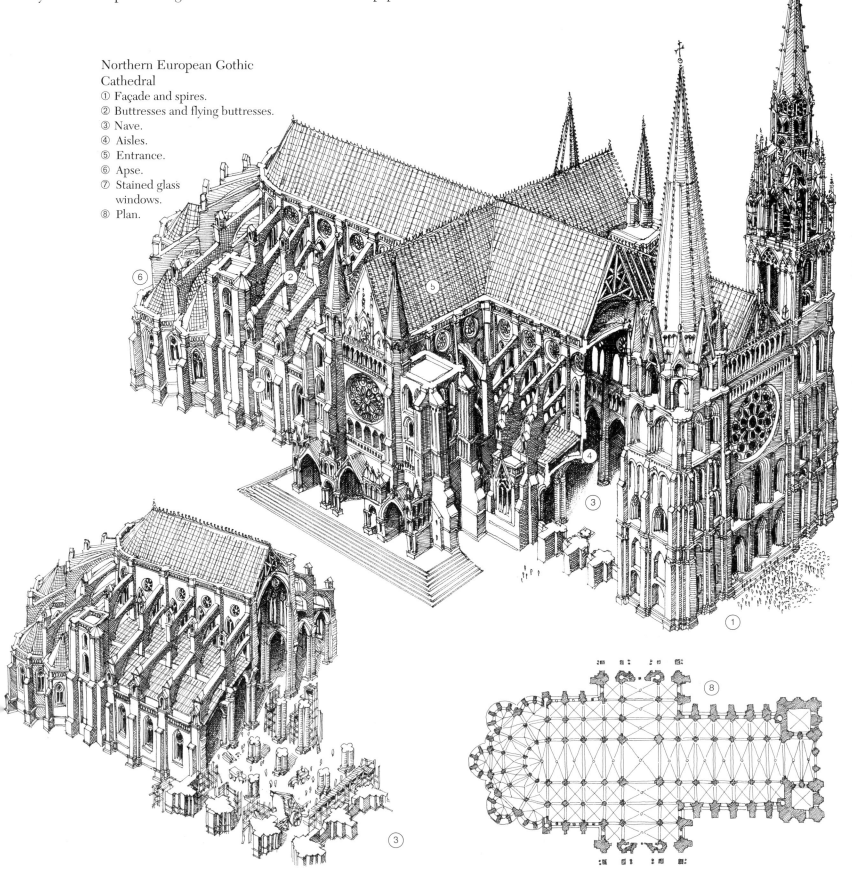

5. A MERCANTILE CITY IN DECLINE: Early Sixteenth Century

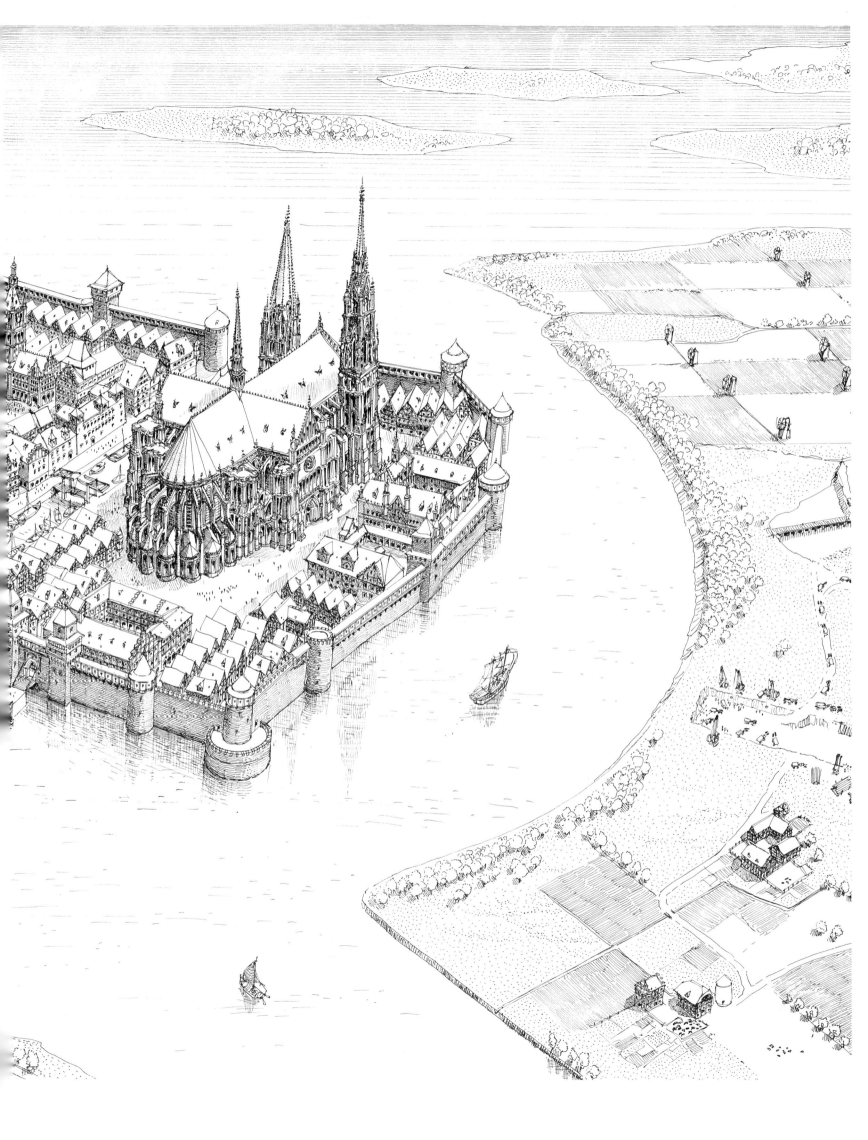

5. A Mercantile City in Decline
Early Sixteenth Century

Throughout the fifteenth century, the medieval city of Lebek grew and prospered. Occasional crises arose, but the city weathered them and, as the sixteenth century opened, continued to erect impressive new structures: the university, the Woolen Cooperative building, a new façade for the Diet. Residential areas on the city's western edge had expanded to the gates of the herring processing plants and shipyards. Three-masted ships of enormous tonnage floated at anchor in the harbor.

The tide of prosperity, however, had already begun to turn. The North Sea herring banks suddenly disappeared, putting the fishing and processing sectors of the economy into crisis. The Scandinavian monarchies, particularly Sweden's, moved to consolidate and expand their power while Russia extended her sphere of influence ever deeper into

1. University
Medieval universities offered few subjects relevant to commerce and industry. The curriculum typically included theology, jurisprudence, canonic law, grammar, rhetoric, Greek, Latin, and medicine. The sciences were considered in theoretical rather than practical terms. Decades would elapse before applied sciences found a place in the course of studies.

2. Company Headquarters and Guildhalls
Lebek's leading guilds and businesses housed themselves in palatial buildings emblematic of their strength and importance. These headquarters contained offices, assembly rooms, files, and archives. Each of Lebek's business enterprises was a highly structured and efficient organization that observed special traditions and festivals under its own proudly displayed banner.

3. Canals, Mills, and Dikes
During the fifteenth century, the struggle against marshes and the sea intensified. Lands chosen for reclamation were enclosed by a high wall or earthwork. On top

of these, windmills were installed. The windmills drove spiral dredges, or Archimedes' screws, that suctioned the water off the land and emptied it into peripheral canals or rivers. Dikes, dams, and locks protected and regulated the complex canal system.

4. Shipyards
By the beginning of the sixteenth century, carracks were being replaced by four-masted galleons whose construction required enormous quantities of lumber, skilled shipwrights, and special equipment.

5. Diet
In the early sixteenth century the original Gothic building was embellished with a Renaissance-style façade.

Port
The port was Lebek's nerve center. Barges, herring trawlers, and ocean-going carracks anchored in the shelter of its palisades. Cargoes destined for nearby warehouses or ships' holds were stacked on the docks.

① Crane.
② Wharf.
③ Bales of woolen cloth and barrels of salt herring.
④ Carrack.
⑤ Herring trawler.

Northern Europe. The power of the free cities was seriously threatened, and the opening of the Americas to European colonization served to weaken it further. As the New World's vast resources were discovered and exploited, traffic along the old medieval trade routes slackened, and the Atlantic became the major conduit for maritime traffic and commerce.

A powerful monarchy absorbed the former duchy of the Lower Leb, and Lebek lost its independence. The city's merchants struggled to adapt to the new conditions and to gain a foothold in the trans-Atlantic trade, but it was no easy task to forge simultaneously a new economic base, political identity, and trade network. A few of Lebek's mariners did venture forth, however, on trade routes to the West Indies.

City life continued at a slackened pace. Lebek's cloth industry benefited from the importation of cheap wool, while many of Lebek's merchants turned their energies to banking. The city's growing financial institutions ensured that a portion of the gold and silver pouring into Europe from the New World would find its way into Lebek's coffers.

The city's struggle with the sea continued and, with the aid of new technology, achieved greater measures of success. Windmills came into general use during the fifteenth century and by the sixteenth century were part of a systematized effort to drain the marshes. Dikes were built to withstand the sea's fury, and canals dug to provide an outlet for the evacuated water. The network of navigable channels was improved, and other public works were undertaken.

House, Early Sixteenth Century
In the early sixteenth century, the houses built for artisans and merchants, although much larger and better equipped than in the past, still conformed to the medieval pattern. Roofs were pitched, and façades were decorated rather than plain. Interior space was exploited for maximum use, and some dwellings had small back gardens.
① Façade.
② Street.
③ Cellar.
④ Ground floor.
⑤ Second floor.

6. WATER: ALLY AND ENEMY: Early Seventeenth Century

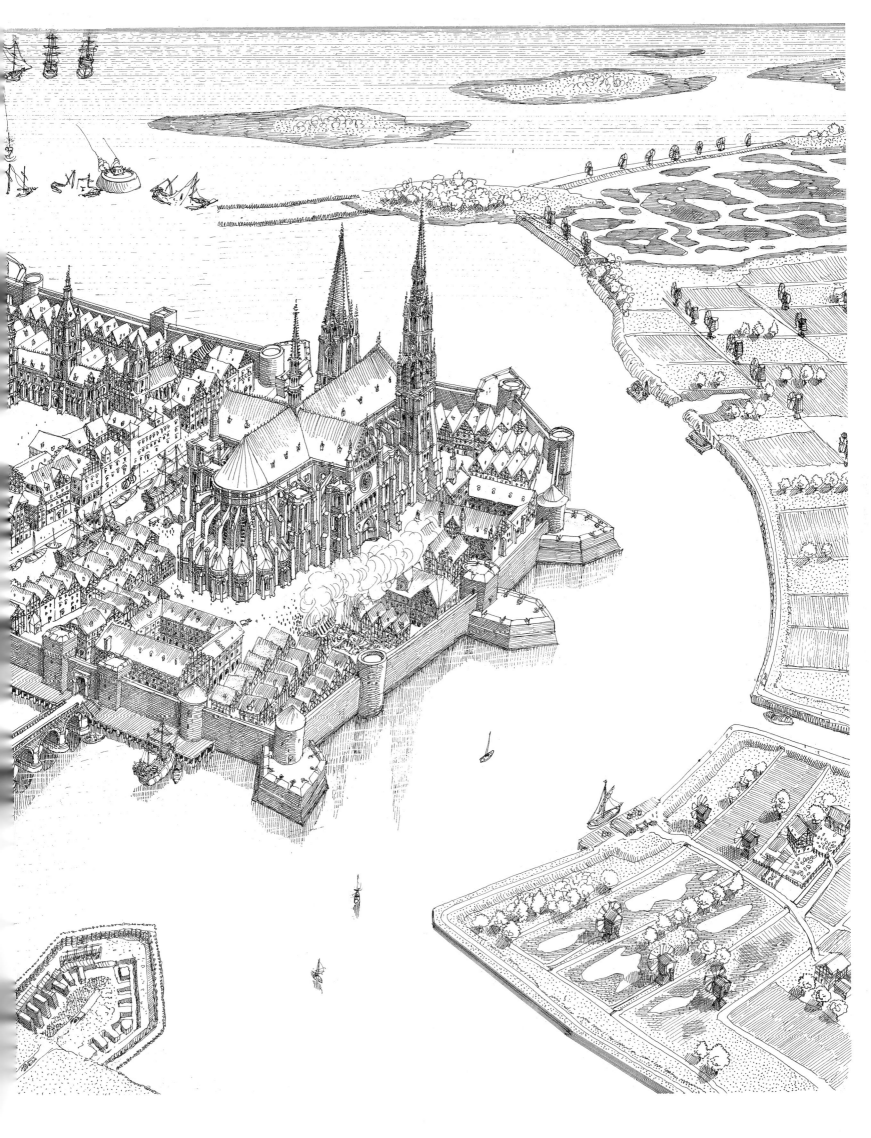

6. Water: Ally and Enemy
Early Seventeenth Century

By the mid-sixteenth century Lebek was beginning to emerge from its lethargy. Its merchants scrambled, along with those of other north coast cities, to gain a foothold in the commerce with the East and West Indies.

In their efforts to capture a share of the lucrative trade, they went so far as to offer aid and refuge to pirates. Lebek's bankers, meanwhile, broadly expanded their services.

The battle against the sea intensified. More dikes were built and additional canals dug. Windmills turned day and night to drain marshes and gain land for cultivation. The growing network of canals, dams, locks, and drawbridges ensured excellent communications between Lebek and the rural districts of the interior. The port also was enlarged and made more secure for the merchant galleons, herring boats, yachts, and coastal vessels moored there. Alongside them floated the pirate ships that, tacitly supported by Lebek's governing bodies, intercepted Spanish convoys transporting gold and silver from the Americas and carried their

1. Windmills
Sixteenth- and seventeenth-century improvements in the design and construction of windmills dramatically increased their efficiency. Groups of windmills worked in concert to drain water from lowland tracts. Both wind- and water-powered mills were used to grind grain into flour.

2. Dike Construction
The first step in a land-reclamation project was to build a circular system of dikes. The soil to build this earthen embankment was taken from lowlands just beyond the proposed perimeter. As the dike rose, the canal that would provide drainage was dug behind it. Timbers and brambles reinforced the finished dike. Drainage windmills turned atop it. Land that lay far below sea level could be drained only by batteries of windmills positioned at successive levels.

3. Flooded Fields
Storms occasionally broke through dikes, causing water to flood reclaimed fields. In times of war, the floodgates of both dikes and dams were intentionally opened. These manmade floods constituted a powerful barrier to invading armies.

4. Fortified Ramparts
The enlarged city wall was built with bastions. From them, the defensive artillery fired on advancing enemies. The walls themselves were low but solid enough to stop an enemy's artillery fire. Broad trenches or moats in front of the walls further impeded the enemy's assaults.

5. Assault Trenches
In order to conquer Lebek, assailants had to breach its walls. They dug deep trenches that advanced on the walls in a zigzag pattern. The attacking artillery sheltered in the trenches. The infantry used the trenches as approaches when staging its assaults.

Battery of Drainage Windmills
Lands far below sea level were drained by groups of windmills acting in concert. Together they raised water to progressively higher canals. The windmills at the highest elevation spilled water into rivers or into dammed canals that were emptied during low tides directly into the sea.

① High-water mark.
② Low-water mark.
③ Dike.
④ Windmill.
⑤ Drainage canal.

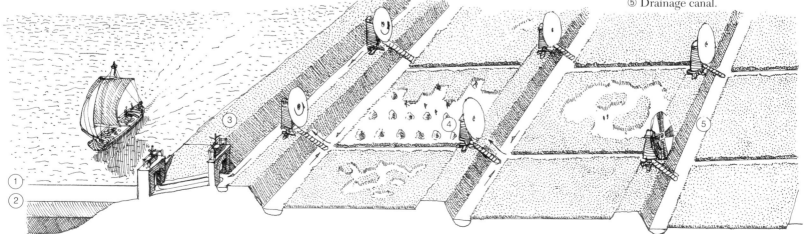

plunder into the port. The city's whaling industry also grew, as sales of whale oil and small whalebones for use in corsets and umbrella frames brought substantial profits.

Within Lebek, redevelopment efforts were resumed. A stone bridge in the Flemish style joined the island city to the mainland for the first time. New districts grew on the city's outskirts, and fortifications were raised to protect the head of the bridge.

Unfortunately, difficult political conditions framed this renewed dynamism. Lebek found itself drawn into the terrible religious wars that convulsed Europe during much of the sixteenth century, only to be followed by the devastating Thirty Years War of the early seventeenth century. Lebek's inhabitants supported the Protestant cause and joined other cities in an uprising against the Holy Roman Empire.

The war exacted a heavy toll. Although the city's militias fought coura-geously, many of its soldiers died in battle. At the beginning of the seventeenth century, the imperial armies began a new offensive intended to put down the rebellion, once and for all. Some cities were sacked and their inhabitants brutally slaughtered.

With an attack on Lebek imminent, the city's military commanders took bold action. They ordered the floodgates of dams and dikes to be opened. Water poured into canals and over fields, transforming the reclaimed lands into bogs. Neither advancing cavalry nor artillery had room to maneuver. The only approach open to the imperial armies was the narrow bridgehead. Lebek's commanders quickly fortified it. Restricted as the attacking armies were to one narrow strip of land, their numerical superiority proved meaningless. Frustrated in their efforts, the invaders withdrew.

The danger past, Lebek's populace turned again to the work of draining the flooded fields and restoring them to cultivation.

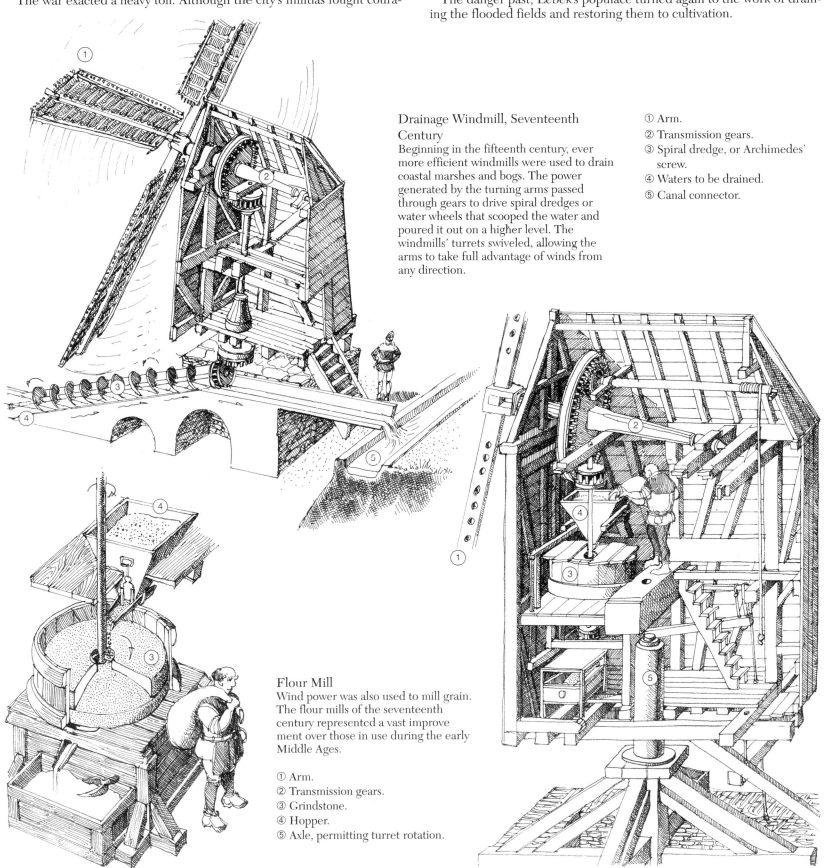

Drainage Windmill, Seventeenth Century

Beginning in the fifteenth century, ever more efficient windmills were used to drain coastal marshes and bogs. The power generated by the turning arms passed through gears to drive spiral dredges or water wheels that scooped the water and poured it out on a higher level. The windmills' turrets swiveled, allowing the arms to take full advantage of winds from any direction.

① Arm.
② Transmission gears.
③ Spiral dredge, or Archimedes' screw.
④ Waters to be drained.
⑤ Canal connector.

Flour Mill

Wind power was also used to mill grain. The flour mills of the seventeenth century represented a vast improve ment over those in use during the early Middle Ages.

① Arm.
② Transmission gears.
③ Grindstone.
④ Hopper.
⑤ Axle, permitting turret rotation.

7. MODERN EXPANSION: Mid-Seventeenth Century

7. Modern Expansion
Mid-Seventeenth Century

By the middle of the seventeenth century, the long wars against the Holy Roman Empire had ended. The duchy of the Lower Leb regained its political independence and united with adjacent provinces to form a principality under a ruling dynasty.

As political conditions stabilized, Lebek turned its considerable energy and resources to commerce. The United Provinces quickly assembled a colonial empire, with bases in both the Far East and the New World. While many of Lebek's citizens migrated to the colonies to establish or supervise businesses, the city's port thrived with the increased trade.

The rarest and most exotic products of half the world now poured into Lebek's wharves: pepper, cinnamon, saffron, ginger, sugar, tobacco, a variety of manufactured goods, and gold and silver. Rather than serve as

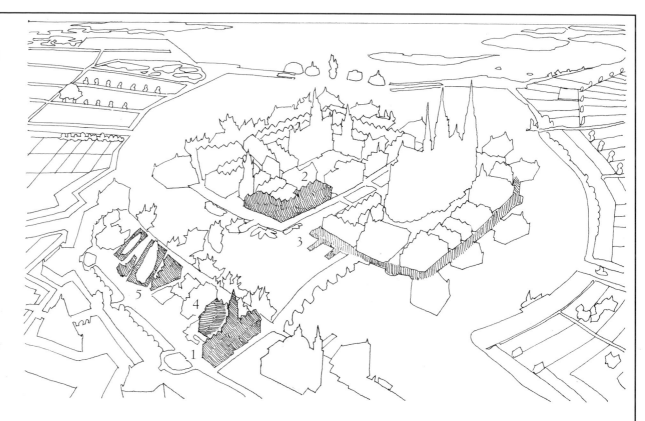

1. Securities Exchange
Lebek's growing financial service industry required an appropriate seat. Gathered under the roof of the exchange were stock and bond traders, insurers, commodities brokers, commercial registries, and archives.

2. New Streets and Buildings
The city's powerful middle class used its prosperity to renovate houses in a grander style. Dwellings were enlarged as much as Lebek's limited space would permit, and richly ornamented façades were added.

3. Docks
The extension of the city's fortified walls provided secure new space for wharves for the growing shipping trade. The supply of space, however, would never equal the demand, and the difficulty of accommodating ships anxious to load and unload cargo speedily remained a problem.

4. Herring Processing Plant
Techniques for preserving fish improved. While traditional salting was still practiced, smoke processing overtook it in popu-larity. Masses of herring were laid out on drying frames. A central hearth supplied the smoke that cured the fish. Smoke processing offered Lebek the additional benefit of freeing it from dependency on outside sources for processing salt.

5. Whale By-Product Processing Plant
Whaling ships generally processed their catches at sea. Animals caught near the port, however, were towed into the estuary for processing in a plant. Whale meat was heated to high temperatures to render fat and oil that had multiple uses in manufacturing.

Façade of a Canalside Street

The city's most desirable commercial streets bordered canals. The waterways permitted easy transfer of cargoes to and from ships and warehouses. The prosperity of these streets was evident in the elaborate façades. As years passed, baroque façades gave way to the neoclassical. A distinctive touch was the use of whimsical finials to disguise the roofs' rain gutters.

a mere market for foreign goods, however, Lebek continued to produce products of its own. Its herring boats plied the most distant stretches of the North and Baltic seas in search of fish, while the whaling industry continued its activities, unabated.

The rise of a formidable new naval power, England, threatened to create problems for Lebek and the United Provinces. Wars were waged over North Sea fishing rights, and the city's powerful fleet participated in the conflicts with success.

Lebek's workshops continued to turn out woolen cloth and, in increasing quantity, finely tooled machinery. As the city extended its physical limits, every square foot of arable land was cultivated. Within the sheltering city walls, the naval shipyards bustled with activity, turning out

more and more ships to protect the valuable trade routes. The deep Leb basin was unexcelled as a launch site for these gigantic vessels.

In another burst of construction activity, a magnificent new building was erected in Lebek's mainland district to house one of Europe's first modern securities exchanges. Virtually all other land within the city limits was occupied by the houses of merchants and artisans. In the old city center, where horizontal expansion was an impossibility, the houses began to grow vertically. The new houses of other districts, with their sharply pitched roofs and profusely ornamented façades, testified to the city's solid middle-class prosperity.

The war-damaged fields, meanwhile, were revitalized and returned to cultivation. Agriculture and dairy farming thrived along the Lower Leb. Cheese production in particular prospered, as Lebek enjoyed one of the most fruitful periods of its history.

Merchant House

Although the middle class formed the backbone of the thriving merchant cities, its members lived in relatively simple dwellings. The scarcity of land in Lebek dictated modest dimensions for the city's attached houses. In compensation for their size, these residences offered a high degree of comfort. Household supplies were stored in cellars or in attics, into which they were hoisted on pulleys attached to upper-story window frames.

① Entrance.
② Kitchen.
③ Drawing room.
④ Study.
⑤ Bedroom.
⑥ Cellar storeroom.
⑦ Attic storeroom.

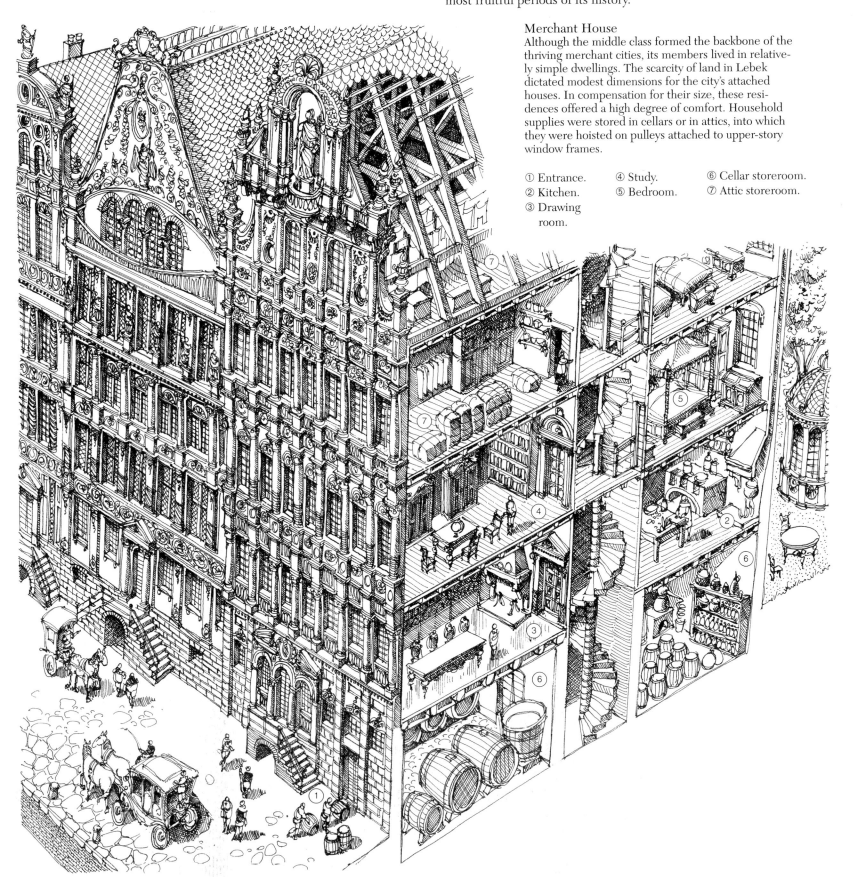

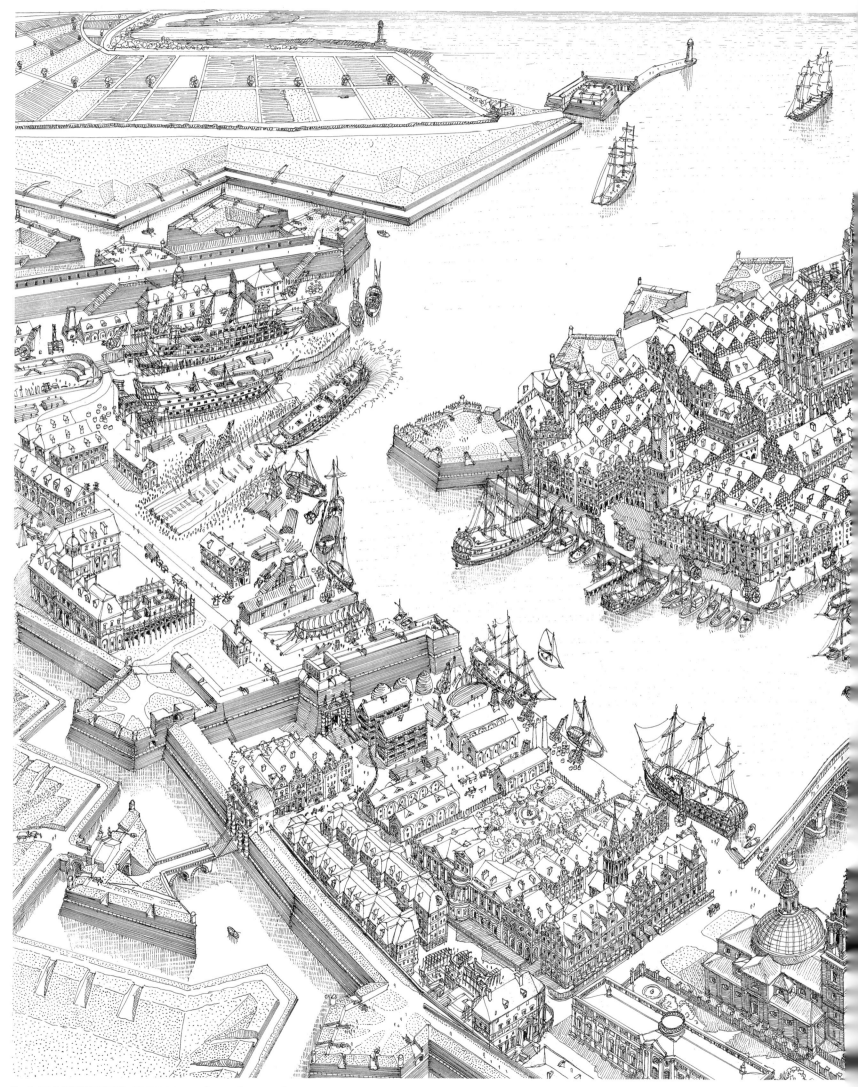

8. A FORTIFIED PORT: Mid-Eighteenth Century

8. A Fortified Port
Mid-Eighteenth Century

During the eighteenth century, a series of complex political changes plunged Northern Europe into a period of prolonged military conflict. Lebek retreated behind its walls and strengthened its defenses. Its heavily reinforced ramparts were topped with fortresses, the design of which followed engineering principles recently introduced by French military engineers.

The city continued to play its ancient role of major port and commercial center, but the new fortifications transformed it into a geopolitically strategic stronghold as well. The United Provinces' naval and merchant marine fleets rode at anchor in the Lebek harbor. The shipbuilding industry continued to flourish as the government increased its demands for huge new warships.

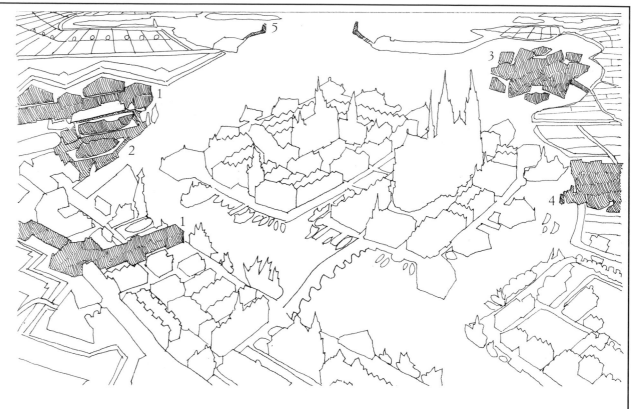

1. Fortified Naval Shipyard
The naval shipyard formed a self-sufficient community, equipped with a variety of warehouses and workshops. Its military function required that it be isolated from the rest of the city by fortified walls.

2. Dry Dock
Costly and complex dry docks made the construction and repair of large vessels possible.

3. Fortresses
During the eighteenth century, engineering advances substantially improved defensive fortifications. Fortresses were erected at strategic locations to guard the flanks and the heights of a stronghold.

4. Coal Docks
The shipping of coal by sea became common practice in the eighteenth century. Vessels endowed with generous holds and sturdy hulls received the coal from elevated hoppers.

5. Lighthouses
Lighthouses and lightships were built to promote safe navigation.

Their beacons assisted vessels in taking their bearings and made

possible safe nighttime entrances and departures from the port.

Shipyard Forge
The large naval shipyard employed hundreds of specialized workers. Carpenters, caulkers, and shipwrights saw to the construction of ships. Rope makers worked in large sheds, producing rope, cable, and cord of every type. Woodcarvers, cabinetmakers, and painters were responsible for the finishing work.

Forge and foundry occupied a position of particular importance. The forge produced every type of utensil used on shipboard, from massive anchors to cupboard hinges. The foundries of some of the larger shipyards cast cannon and all varieties of small firearms.

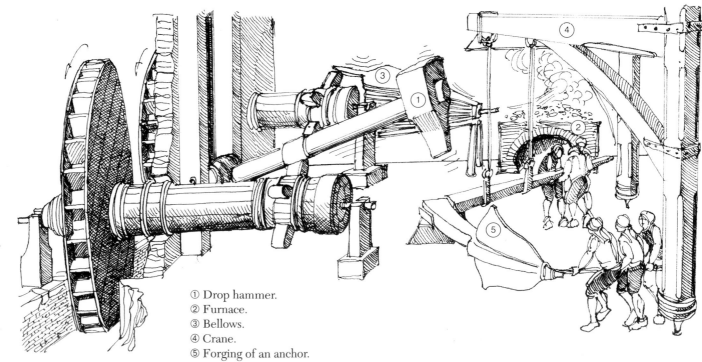

① Drop hammer.
② Furnace.
③ Bellows.
④ Crane.
⑤ Forging of an anchor.

The city built an enormous naval shipyard whose fortifications protected and isolated it, as much from the city's civilian populace as from enemies without. Warehouses and workshops of every type provided the services and equipment indispensable to the maintenance and provisioning of warships. A forge produced anchors and hardware. A ropemaker's shop turned out top-quality lines for rigging and cordage.

The shipyard possessed slips designed for the construction of conventional ships, but its most valuable component was the gigantic dry dock. Naval shipwrights used the dry dock secondarily for construction, but primarily for the repair of large-tonnage ships. Once the ship was inside, the dry dock's sluice gates were closed, and the water was drained by pumps and water wheels. Caulkers and shipwrights then had easy access to all parts of the vessel.

During this period, the woolen textile industry was also transformed. Individual workshops were replaced by large factories. Although the factories used the same techniques as had the workshops, the simple concentration of workers and production processes within their walls marked the end of the era of artisans and the beginning of the Industrial Age.

Lebek was also indirectly influenced by the advances in metallurgy that introduced coal-burning blast-furnace processes into the production of iron and steel. Coal barges arrived daily in the port from the interior coal fields. Once in port, the coal was transferred to specially designed ships that transported it to the iron- and steel-processing sites.

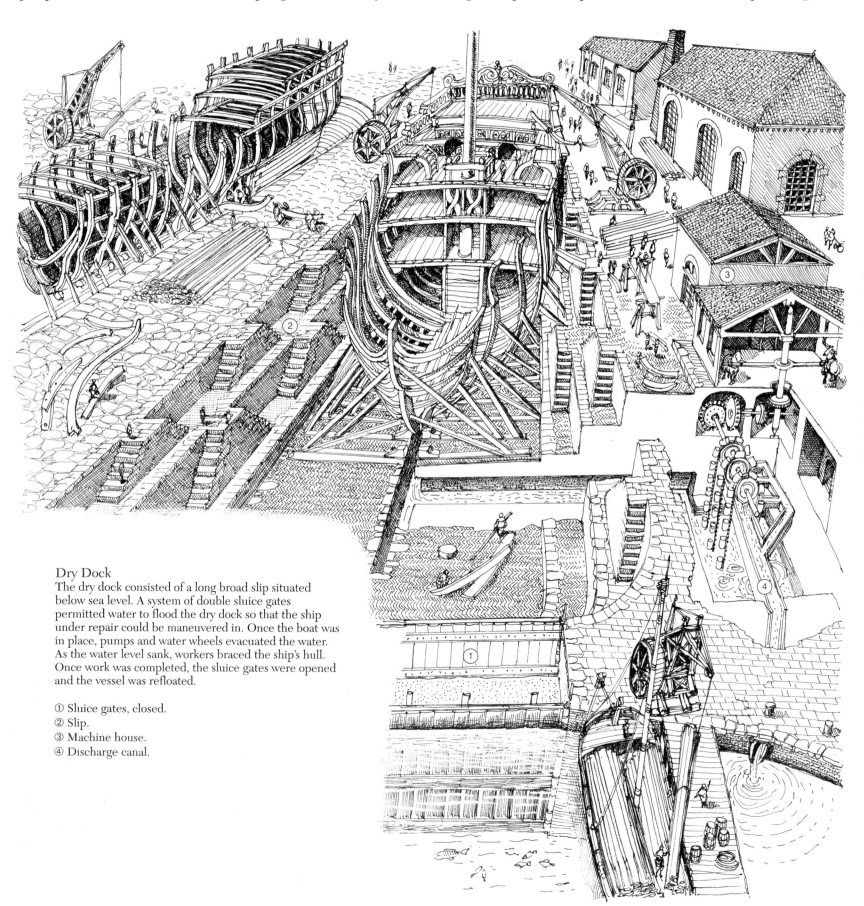

Dry Dock
The dry dock consisted of a long broad slip situated below sea level. A system of double sluice gates permitted water to flood the dry dock so that the ship under repair could be maneuvered in. Once the boat was in place, pumps and water wheels evacuated the water. As the water level sank, workers braced the ship's hull. Once work was completed, the sluice gates were opened and the vessel was refloated.

① Sluice gates, closed.
② Slip.
③ Machine house.
④ Discharge canal.

9. THE SLOW TRANSITION: Early Nineteenth Century

9. The Slow Transition
Early Nineteenth Century

During the last decades of the eighteenth century and the first of the nineteenth, Lebek gathered strength for the period of frenetic expansion that would follow shortly. Liberal revolutions were transforming the political face of Europe, but it was the scientific and technological advances that dramatically altered the continent's urban landscape. Chief among these were the development of the iron and steel industry, the first experiments with steam engines, and the progressive mechanization of the textile industry, all signaling the greater changes to come.

As Lebek continued to grow, the strategic value of its city walls declined. Far from protecting city and port, the walls served now only to hinder their growth. Salt fish and textile manufacturing remain important industries, but the port's commerce also expanded in new direc-

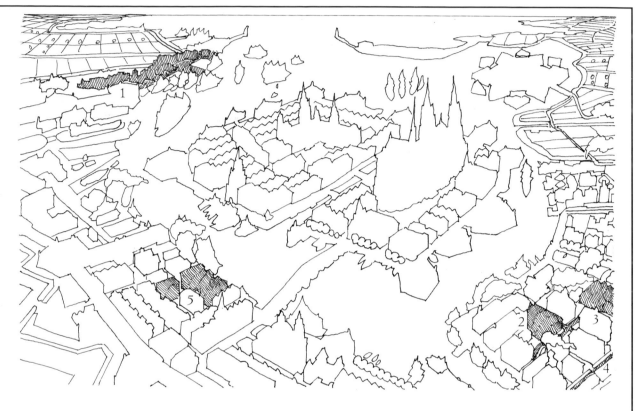

1. New Docks
As maritime traffic from Europe's colonial empires grew, Lebek's merchants built additional docks able to accommodate increasingly larger ships. The maritime quarter that grew up around the docks furnished every type of service and provision required by mercantile and naval ships and their crews.

2. Factories
Factories created large numbers of newly salaried employees. Rather than paying hourly wages to managers and supervisors, the factory owner guaranteed them a fixed sum of money in exchange for their work. While the method of paying some employees changed, the factories' production processes, machinery, and power sources did not. Meanwhile, the competition from large, mechanized factories put some centuries-old guilds, particularly those in the textile industry, out of business.

3. Working-Class Districts
*The factory replaced the fortified castle and the cathedral as the new center of urban development. Working-class districts sprang up around the factory gates, and in some of the city's most depressed quarters tene-*ments rose higher and higher to accommodate growing numbers of urban poor.

4. Elevated Canal
The rivers and streams of the surrounding lowlands flowed too slowly to power hydraulic machinery. Factory owners built elevated canals to channel water from distant mountainous regions and create a flow powerful enough to activate factory water wheels. These canals also powered a variety of mills built along their courses.

5. New Buildings within the Old City
Privately financed buildings rose within the old city: naval academies, surgical schools, shipping and trade councils, banks, nobles' palaces, and the mansions of wealthy merchants and industrialists. Their design, for the most part, reflected the neoclassical style that was then popular throughout Europe.

① Hydraulic wheel.
② Workshop.
③ Skylights, to provide natural lighting.
④ Bell, to signal work hours.

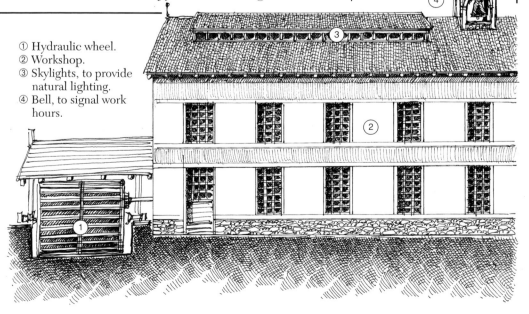

Textile Plant
Large textile factories, primarily for the spinning of cotton, began to appear in Northern Europe at the close of the eighteenth century and the opening of the nineteenth. The factory's hydraulic wheel activated gears that powered drive shafts positioned throughout the factory. Power was transmitted through these shafts to belts, and onward to the various machines of the spinning process: carder, gin, spool, and above all the mule-jenny, a modern device capable of spinning quickly and efficiently.

tions. As the demand for coal increased, an uninterrupted file of barges ferried it downriver from the interior coal fields to the port. An increasing number of ships originating in distant European ports and in the United Provinces' overseas possessions arrived in Lebek laden with exotic products: tea, coffee, sugar, precious woods, and above all, raw cotton. Cotton processing quickly became one of the city's primary industries. New factories spun cotton fiber into thread and wove the thread into cloth; the finished cloth was exported to markets all over the world.

Lack of space at Lebek's center made urban redevelopment a near impossibility. Some houses and public buildings were renovated, nevertheless, and new offices were built by increasingly powerful banks. Outside the city walls, additional docks were built to provide space for increased shipping traffic. A colorful district sprang up in the docks' immediate vicinity. Its clustered taverns, shops, rooming houses, service agencies, and warehouses catered to every need of the mercantile and naval fleets and their crews.

The new cotton industry was forced by the city's lack of building space to site its factories outside Lebek's walls. Elevated canals originating in the mountainous region to the south were built to provide hydraulic power to run automated spinning wheels in the factories.

Industry was rapidly overtaking trade as the city's primary economic base. As the first working-class districts grew up next to the factories, Lebek began to assume the shape of a modern industrial city and port.

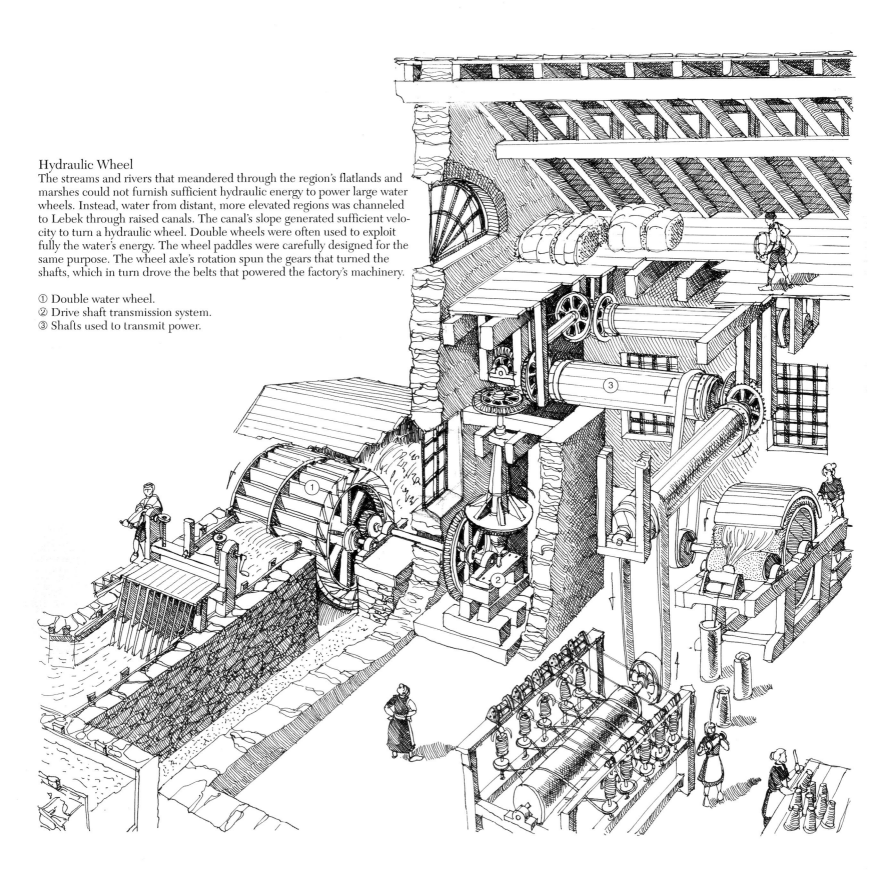

Hydraulic Wheel
The streams and rivers that meandered through the region's flatlands and marshes could not furnish sufficient hydraulic energy to power large water wheels. Instead, water from distant, more elevated regions was channeled to Lebek through raised canals. The canal's slope generated sufficient velocity to turn a hydraulic wheel. Double wheels were often used to exploit fully the water's energy. The wheel paddles were carefully designed for the same purpose. The wheel axle's rotation spun the gears that turned the shafts, which in turn drove the belts that powered the factory's machinery.

① Double water wheel.
② Drive shaft transmission system.
③ Shafts used to transmit power.

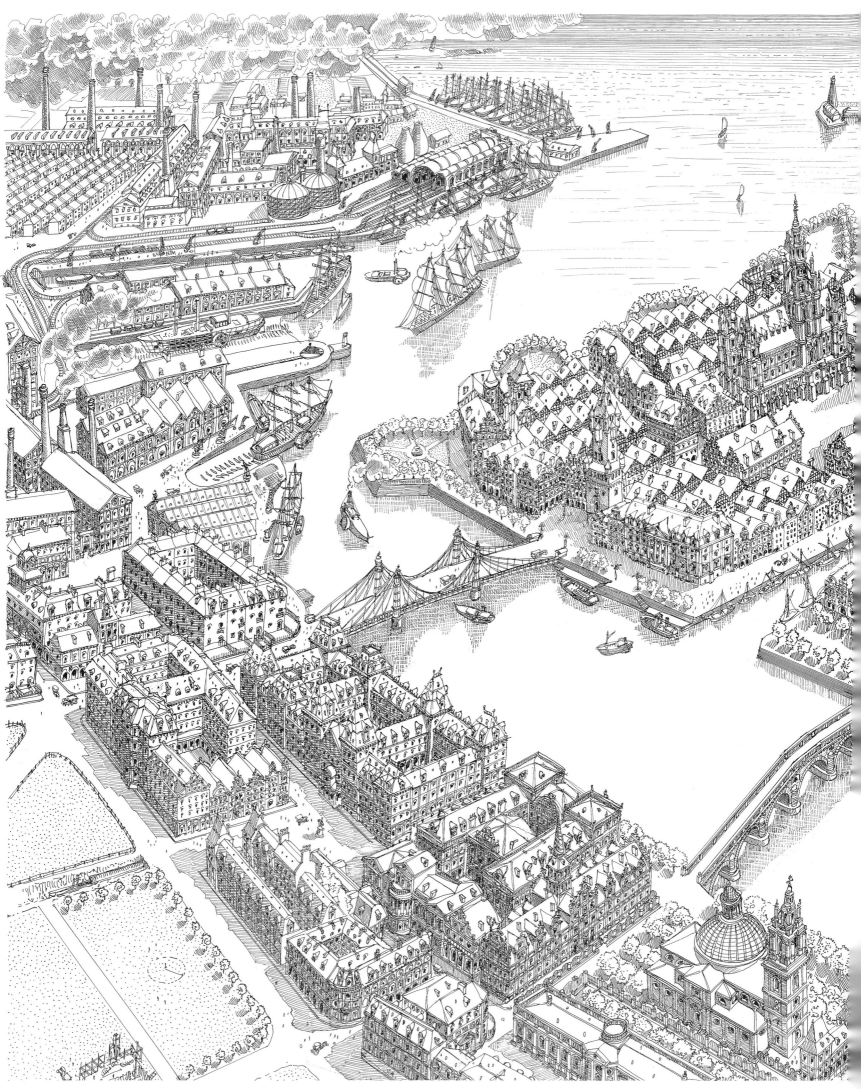

10. BURSTS OF STEAM: Mid-Nineteenth Century

10. Bursts of Steam
Mid-Nineteenth Century

In the mid-nineteenth century, the steam engine ushered Lebek into a period of frantic change. Old factories adopted steam as their standard energy source while new steam-powered plants multiplied in the region. Farms on the city's perimeter were moved farther and farther back to make way for the industrial expansion. Lebek's skyline was now distinguished by its dozens of towering smokestacks.

Working-class districts, laid out in blocklike tracts around the new factories, provided housing for the thousands of laborers who had left the fields in search of industrial jobs in the city. Older quarters also felt the effects of industrialization. The fortified walls were demolished. The naval shipyard, now totally obsolete, was razed and its lands were absorbed, along with the older suburbs, into new industrial zones.

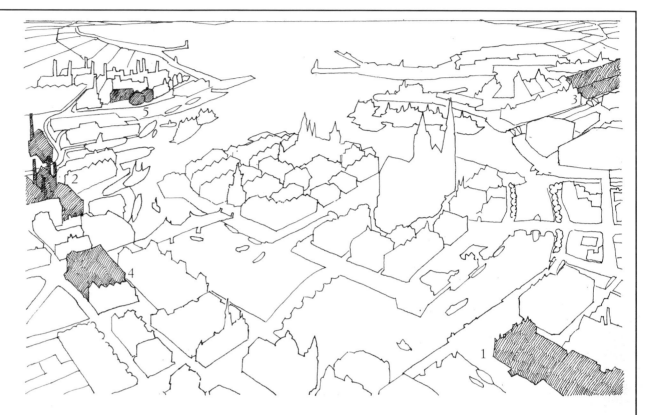

1. Railroad Stations
The extension of railroad lines into the city made the redevelopment of certain old districts a necessity. Trains provided cheap and rapid transport and guaranteed swift transfer of perishable goods from the port.

2. Steam-Powered Factories
The construction of large, steam-powered plants radically altered the urban landscape. The mechanized manufacturing process led to spectacular production increases.

3. Working-Class Districts
The owners of factories frequently built housing for workers near the plants. These districts of rectilinear streets and identical row houses became a leading characteristic of the industrial city.

4. Residential Neighborhoods
Far from the smoke of the factories and the port's activity, corporations, banks, and other commercial enterprises headquartered their operations in comfortable middle- and upper-middle-class neighborhoods.

5. Gasworks
An underground pipe system conveyed gas to the lamps of the city's streetlights. Gas fixtures were also common in the homes of the well-to-do and in the majority of factories. Artificial illumination permitted factory night shifts that kept production lines operating twenty-four hours a day. Factories not connected to the city gas lines acquired gas-storage tanks of their own.

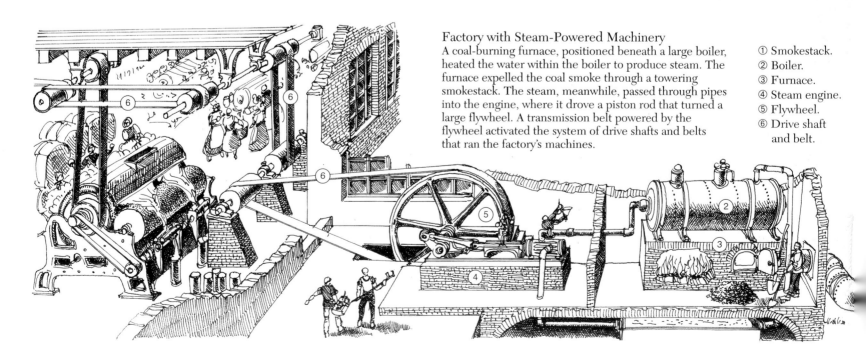

Factory with Steam-Powered Machinery
A coal-burning furnace, positioned beneath a large boiler, heated the water within the boiler to produce steam. The furnace expelled the coal smoke through a towering smokestack. The steam, meanwhile, passed through pipes into the engine, where it drove a piston rod that turned a large flywheel. A transmission belt powered by the flywheel activated the system of drive shafts and belts that ran the factory's machines.

① Smokestack.
② Boiler.
③ Furnace.
④ Steam engine.
⑤ Flywheel.
⑥ Drive shaft and belt.

Iron produced in modern ironworks became the primary construction material, particularly for bridges. Railroad lines extended their routes into the city center and the port. Their passenger and freight cars complemented the traditional river barges in offering rapid, efficient transportation to passengers and, more critically, to freight.

Steam power also had a decisive influence on navigation. While the makers of traditional, wooden sailing ships attempted to hold their share of the market by improving the speed and overall performance of their vessels, their replacement by modern iron-hulled streamships was inevitable.

Lebek's port was ill equipped to handle the new ships, and its facilities were totally inadequate for servicing the maritime traffic that was increasing by geometric progression. New wharves and warehouses were built along the estuary's seaward side. The port authorities, meanwhile, dredged canals and cutoffs that would allow them to control the river's flow into the estuary and regulate its seasonal fluctuations.

Lebek's growing number of financiers, factory owners, and professionals, as well as its newly wealthy upper middle class and prosperous middle class, all contributed to the rapid expansion of the city's residential districts. At the same time, Lebek provided its inhabitants with important new services. Coal was processed in a central plant to produce gas both for domestic consumption and to power metropolitan streetlights. A sewer system was built, and as a result of the most important public works project, a pipeline from the inland regions furnished the city with running water and made possible the abandonment of unsatisfactory phreatic wells.

Housing for Workers

In the immediate vicinity of large factories, working-class districts arose. These planned districts were laid out along rectilinear grids. The housing was standardized to keep construction costs low. The resultant row houses contained scant living space and in many cases lacked even the most primitive indoor plumbing facilities.

① Façade.
② Dining room.
③ Kitchen.
④ Bedrooms.
⑤ Coal bin.
⑥ Lavatory.
⑦ Ground-floor plan.
⑧ Second-floor plan.

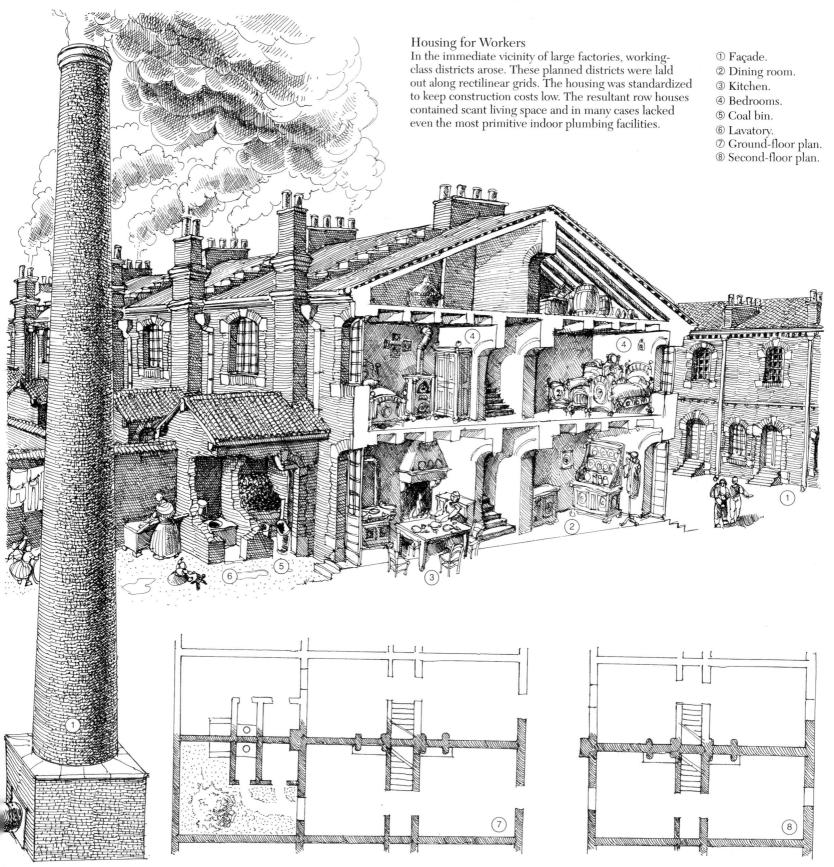

11. A MAJOR PORT EXPANDS: Early Twentieth Century

11. A Major Port Expands
Early Twentieth Century

With the dawn of the new century, the pace of Lebek's industrialization only accelerated. The mass production of electricity as an alternative or supplemental energy source to steam and the diffusion of combustion engines were two developments that opened new possibilities to industry. Electricity, for example, permitted the industrial sector to decentralize, as plants and factories grew less dependent on coal distribution systems.

Lebek, already an important industrial center and port, now assumed the leadership of a region rich in mines and iron- and steelworks: the thriving Upper Leb. As the port achieved increasing importance in international communications and trade, Lebek's diverse roles as industrial producer, marketplace, and transport center were reinforced.

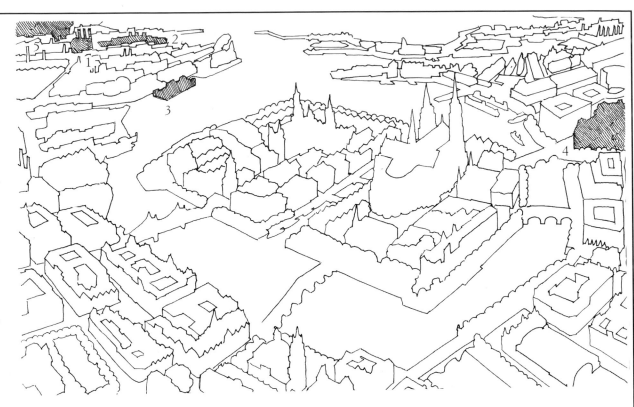

1. Electrical Generating Plant
In large cities electrical generators were built to supply current to the metropolitan area and its suburbs.

2. Naval Shipyards
Disputes over colonial possessions created a demand for ever larger battleships. The great naval shipyards were responsible for the design and construction of all types of war vessels.

3. "Floating" Dry Docks
These repair facilities could be submerged to permit the entry of a ship, and raised to lift the ship from the water for repair work. They made possible the repair and construction of large-tonnage vessels.

4. Hospitals and Other Public Buildings
Growth brought increased services. New hospitals, schools, fire stations, trolley lines, libraries, and museums dotted the urban landscape.

5. Reclaimed Lands
New construction and engineering techniques took advantage of concrete and steel. Both were widely used in the construction of buildings, bridges, canals, and dikes. Reinforced concrete produced structures of great solidity.

Cast-Iron Buildings
Advances in the iron and steel industry provided a ready supply of cheap building materials. The use of cast iron reached massive proportions. Iron beams replaced wooden ones in most buildings, while it also became the preferred building material for support columns, balustrades, and stairways. An architectural style that was literally a celebration of cast iron and its properties evolved. It was used prominently in the construction of such showcase buildings as central markets, concert halls, and auditoriums, as well as of warehouses and industrial hangars.

Two large electrical generator plants furnished power to Lebek's homes and industry. A system of modern trolley lines provided inexpensive transportation within the city while the first automobiles and trucks circulated in the streets. Working-class districts continued to grow as did middle-class neighborhoods. Spectacular new buildings — the headquarters of large banks, maritime companies, and insurers — stood out in the urban landscape.

The port, Lebek's vital link with the Upper Leb, underwent successive enlargements. New wharves shared the harbor with shipyards and with modern "floating" dry docks in which ship repairs were performed. Giant coal storehouses and oil depositories were added to the existing waterfront structures to supply fuel to the new oil-powered boats.

Lebek's naval tradition revived with a fury during this period. The city struggled, along with several other European colonial powers, to maintain control of its overseas empire. The navy added a number of large warships to its fleet and built a dry dock capable of berthing such enormous armored battleships as Dreadnoughts, the most technically advanced warships of the day. As in earlier periods, the naval shipyard and its workshops employed hundreds of laborers.

Meanwhile, the city government turned, again, to land reclamation projects. Civil engineers directed the painstaking construction of the coastal barriers and dikes that permitted them gradually to wrest land from the sea. Huge new parcels of land were added to those already under cultivation, while antiquated windmills were replaced by powerful pumping stations, and older dikes were reinforced with concrete and steel.

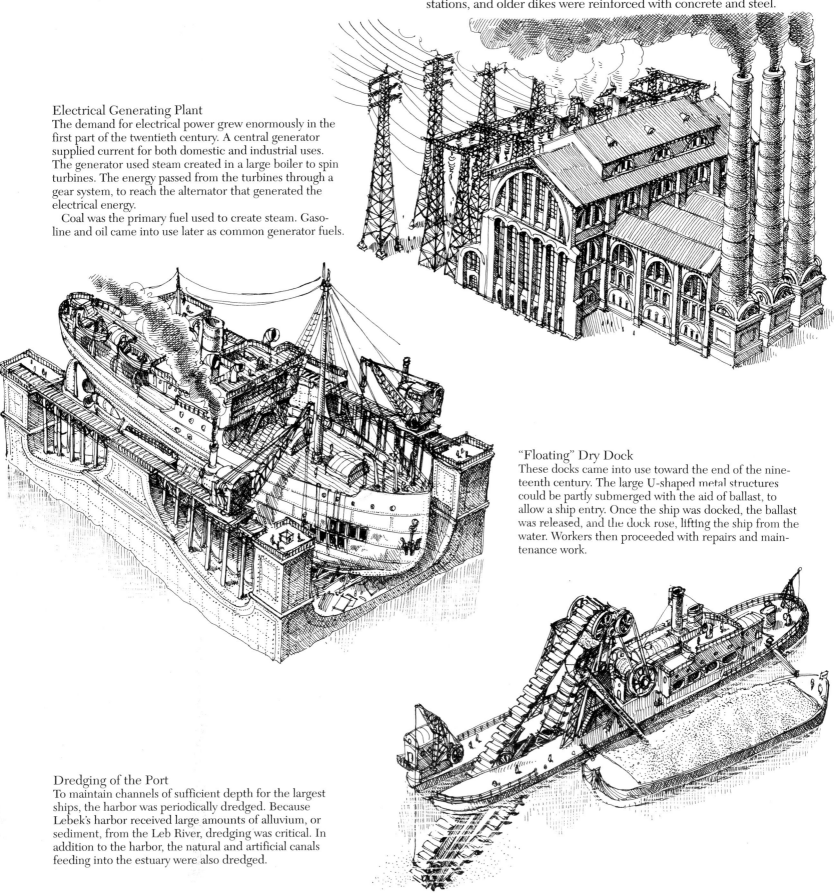

Electrical Generating Plant
The demand for electrical power grew enormously in the first part of the twentieth century. A central generator supplied current for both domestic and industrial uses. The generator used steam created in a large boiler to spin turbines. The energy passed from the turbines through a gear system, to reach the alternator that generated the electrical energy.

Coal was the primary fuel used to create steam. Gasoline and oil came into use later as common generator fuels.

"Floating" Dry Dock
These docks came into use toward the end of the nineteenth century. The large U-shaped metal structures could be partly submerged with the aid of ballast, to allow a ship entry. Once the ship was docked, the ballast was released, and the dock rose, lifting the ship from the water. Workers then proceeded with repairs and maintenance work.

Dredging of the Port
To maintain channels of sufficient depth for the largest ships, the harbor was periodically dredged. Because Lebek's harbor received large amounts of alluvium, or sediment, from the Leb River, dredging was critical. In addition to the harbor, the natural and artificial canals feeding into the estuary were also dredged.

12. WAR AND A NEW BEGINNING: 1940s

12. War and a New Beginning
1940s

During the first third of the twentieth century, although Lebek's harbor and industrial facilities continued to expand, growth occurred at a more relaxed pace than in the period immediately preceding it. Tranquillity ended in the late 1930s, however, when war broke out in Europe.

Lebek, which had escaped the misfortunes of the First World War, was not as fortunate during the Second. World War II quickly became the most tragic period in the city's long history. Lebek was subjected to repeated aerial bombardments. In a single night, incendiary bombs destroyed all the wooden houses of the city's most ancient quarter. Fire companies and army units, unable to control the blazes, looked on helplessly while large portions of the city center burned to the ground.

Lebek's industrial plants and factories, instantly turned over to war

1. Coal Depositories
Large coal-storage facilities were built during the first half of the twentieth century. The large coal stores were required to meet the increasing demand for this inexpensive fuel that powered, among other things, the motors of diesel ships and automobiles.

2. Bombed-out Districts
Powerful incendiary bombs could, in a matter of seconds, reduce entire urban neighborhoods to ashes. The enemy sought to destroy civilian morale through its policy of relentless bombing raids.

3. Dry Dock
Enormous dry docks for the construction and repair of large vessels held a place of great importance in the city's shipyards. A system of gates and pumps regulated water levels and could eliminate water altogether from the dock. Once work was completed, the gates opened, and the ship was refloated and guided out of the dry dock into open water.

4. Antiaircraft Defenses
Antiaircraft batteries were organized to defend Lebek's citizens. Fighter planes, captive barrage balloons, and antiaircraft emplacements all were employed to combat the enemy aircraft.

5. Bomb Shelters and Field Hospitals
Field hospitals were built or improvised to provide care to the civilian wounded.

Bomb Shelter, Cross Section

Bomb shelters provided refuge during air attacks. Cellars, warehouses, and subway stations served as shelters, and new facilities were built. The shelter's entrance was protected by sandbags; the roof was built of steel, concrete, or paving stones. Shelters were furnished with latrines, electrical generators, supplies of food and water, and medical facilities.

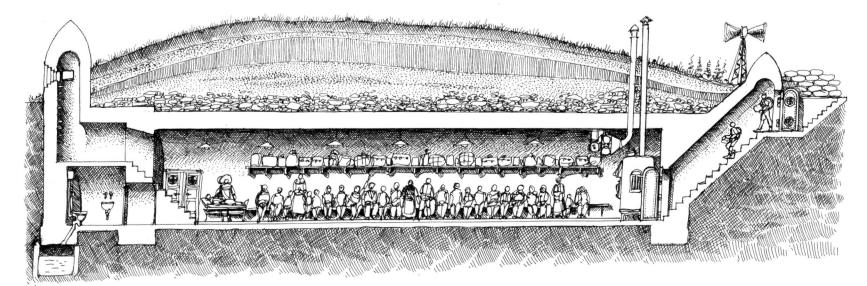

production, were also targeted for major bombing raids, as were the naval shipyards. Bombs completely destroyed the port's immense dry dock and burned the coal depositories. The battleships and merchant vessels that foundered during the bombing raids rested on the harbor bottom, creating hazards to navigation and in some cases completely blocking entry to the port.

Lebek was, during the war's darkest days, the image of utter ruin. Formerly thriving districts were reduced to piles of rubble. The once-proud port was a mass of mangled ironwork and steel, while above the harbor's surface rose the superstructures of sunken vessels.

Hundreds of Lebek's citizens died, either on battlefields or during the bombardments, and the city's misfortunes did not end there. Bombardments of dikes caused flooding over large tracts of reclaimed land. The loss of cultivated fields severely damaged the city's agricultural base. The people themselves were forced to blow up other dikes and bridges deliberately in an effort to slow the advance of enemy armored divisions by flooding additional fields.

Despite the tragedies and hardships, Lebek's people did not lose heart. At the height of the conflict, they began to draw up plans for the reconstruction of the city and port, so that as soon as the war ended, rebuilding could begin. Under these plans, the city would expropriate destroyed properties. Property owners, if they survived, would be indemnified at real estate prices prevailing immediately before the war. The city would, thus, become the proprietor of its own ruined districts, and could recruit engineers and planners to design a less congested and more humane urban environment.

On the first day of peace, despite shortages of every type of commodity and resource, the work of Lebek's reconstruction began.

Antiaircraft Batteries
To combat aerial bombing attacks, antiaircraft emplacements were positioned at strategic points throughout the city. Advance positions relayed warnings of approaching enemy aircraft and provided the artillery with a count of the aircraft and the coordinates of their probable destination. Air-raid sirens alerted civilians to take refuge in shelters. In the case of a night attack, all lights in the city were extinguished, and the antiaircraft gunners used searchlights to locate and target enemy planes.

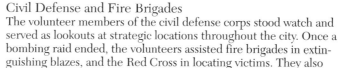

Civil Defense and Fire Brigades
The volunteer members of the civil defense corps stood watch and served as lookouts at strategic locations throughout the city. Once a bombing raid ended, the volunteers assisted fire brigades in extinguishing blazes, and the Red Cross in locating victims. They also took on the often dangerous task of clearing away rubble.

13. MEGALOPOLIS: 1960s

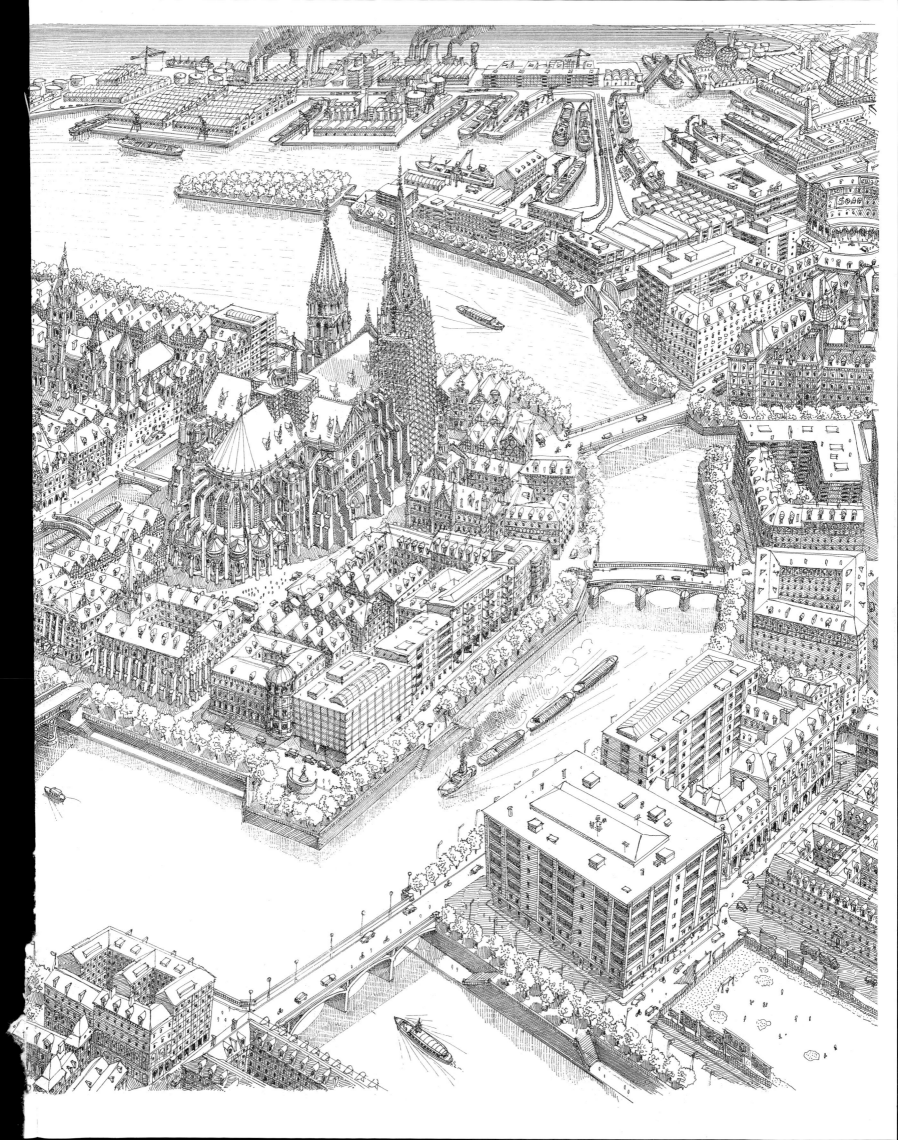

13. Megalopolis
1960s

The postwar years were characterized by feverish activity as all Europe struggled to recover from the war's devastation. The Great Powers contributed both capital goods and financial assistance, but it was the European peoples' hard work and determination that drove and sustained the new period of development.

Lebek, too, began to rebuild furiously. Within a few months, the harbor had been cleared, and gradually the wharves were rebuilt. Maritime traffic and trade resumed, at first on a small scale and then in earnest. In the 1950s the totally reconstructed port began a new phase of expansion.

The city, meanwhile, was cleared of ruins, and urban planners and engineers set about creating practical and appealing districts in their place. Central-city industrial plants that had been destroyed during the

1. Commercial and Service Center
New business districts rose in formerly run-down zones.

2. Industrial Parks
The industrial plants of the central city, which had for the most part been destroyed by the war, were rebuilt in sites on the city's outskirts. The city provided all the services required to guarantee their efficient operation.

3. Satellite Cities
To provide living space for a growing population, districts resembling miniature cities were built on the urban periphery.

4. Cultural and Athletic Facilities
Public athletic fields, sports centers, and swimming pools, as well as libraries, museums, and theaters notably enhanced metropolitan life.

5. Railroad and Highway Improvements
The expansion of the city's physi-

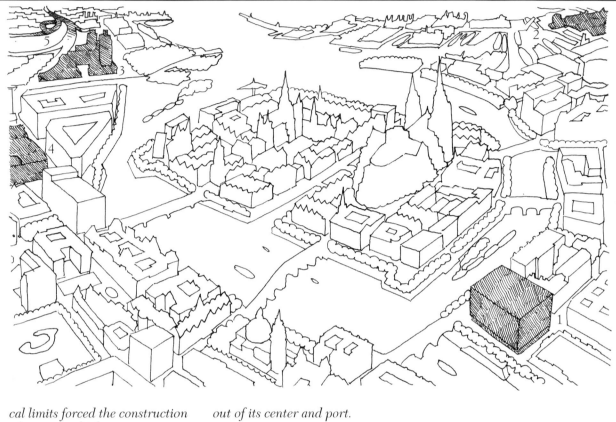

cal limits forced the construction of new superhighways to ensure the free flow of traffic into and out of its center and port.

High-Rise Apartment Buildings
In the majority of the new districts, as well as in some parts of the city center, multistoried apartment buildings rose in large numbers. These high-rises usually followed standard plans and frequently made use of prefabricated construction materials. The rationale for this type of structure was its ability to exploit vertical space in order to create hundreds of reasonably priced units in the confines of its urban site.

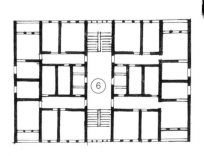

war were rebuilt in outlying areas so that their former sites could be used for the construction of new residential and commercial districts. Railroad lines that obstructed renewal efforts were diverted and linked to the port by more practical routes. As automobile and truck traffic increased, the city adopted appropriate regulatory measures. These revisions of the urban landscape reduced congestion and invested the city with a new graciousness, visible in its broad avenues, public parks and gardens, theaters, museums, and sports facilities.

As the 1960s began, all of industrial Europe entered a period of major economic expansion that boosted both the quantity and quality of its industries. Lebek was scarcely rebuilt when it began to expand its limits again. Industrial parks were financed and built on the city's outskirts, while new wharves, warehouses, and shipyards extended the port and its districts ever farther toward the sea. The port's latest addition was a new petroleum refinery, situated near the mouth of the Leb. Commodities

brokers and producers anxious to move goods in and out of the port could make use of either the traditional barge system or the new rail and highway systems.

New working-class districts, characterized by enormous blocklike apartment buildings, grew up near the industrial zones on the city's outskirts. In contrast to the slums that rose on the peripheries of cities in some other regions of Europe, Lebek's working-class neighborhoods were provided with basic city services.

The city, determined to match growth with improvements in the quality of its citizens' lives, built new hospitals, schools, sports fields, and cultural centers. However, as Lebek grew from major metropolitan area to center of an expanding megalopolis, new problems threatened: pollution, congestion, deterioration of highways and the service infrastructure, plus the multitude of social problems common to all major cities.

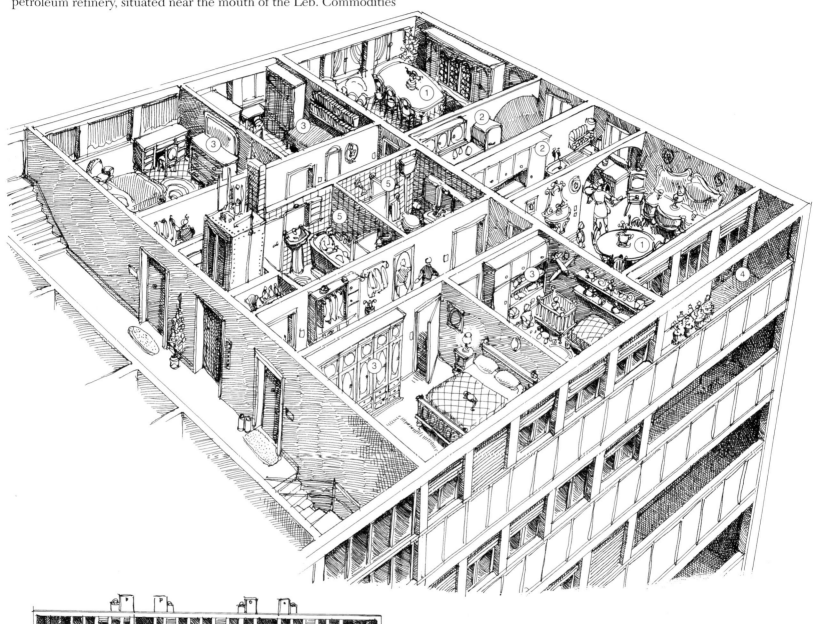

Life in One Thousand Square Feet
In contrast to the dwellings of earlier periods, high-rise apartments were extraordinarily small, rarely exceeding one thousand square feet. In compensation, they offered a high degree of comfort, including such amenities as full electrical power, central heating, telephone and gas service, and assorted electrical appliances that eased domestic chores and promoted leisure time.

① Dining room.
② Kitchen.
③ Bedroom.
④ Terrace.
⑤ Bathroom.
⑥ Floor plan.

14. LOOKING SEAWARD, AGAIN: Late Twentieth Century

14. Looking Seaward, Again
Late Twentieth Century

By the close of the twentieth century, Lebek had achieved a striking balance between its commercial/industrial interests and the needs and comforts of its citizens. In spite of its enormous size, the quality of life in Lebek was generally high.

Contributing to changes in urban life were the economic transformations of the 1970s and 1980s. Industry, Lebek's economic base since the nineteenth century, declined in importance as the city's economy became service based. A number of multinational firms, engaged in global businesses of every sort, established headquarters in Lebek. The city's prosperity drove up costs, spurring some light industries to move to ever more distant outlying areas, or even to countries where labor was cheaper. Lebek became one of Europe's leading business and financial centers,

1. Supertanker Piers
Customs and drayage formalities were begun before the tanker entered the harbor. Once docked, the vessel's oil was transferred to storage tanks.

2. Container Cargo Wharves
Container shipping was extremely popular in the late twentieth century. Specially designed cranes hoisted the enormous containers, or crates, onto and off of the ships, designed solely to convey container cargoes.

3. Warehouses and Grain Silos
The port was equipped with storage facilities to accommodate a variety of cargoes. The enormous silos that stood out on the harbor line, for example, provided storage space for wheat, soybeans, and other grains.

4. Land Access to the Port
Railroads and highways allowed tractor-trailer trucks and freight cars to transport goods easily between the port and inland points of destination or origin.

5. Marine Barriers
Enormous sea walls were built to protect the reclaimed lowlands from storm waters and flooding.

These dikes and barriers included sluiceways that could be

closed when sea levels rose.

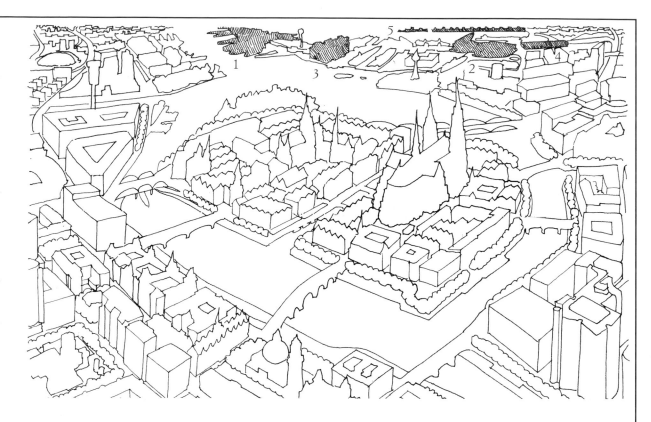

Container Port
Containers offered a convenient way to transport the most varied types of cargoes quickly and securely. Customs agents gave container contents only the most cursory inspection, both in the port of origin and in that of destination. The cargo remained protected throughout the voyage, inside the huge metal container crates. Container dimensions were standardized, and container cargo ships, cranes, trailer trucks, and railroad freight cars were all designed to correspond to them. Transfer of container cargoes was, thus, highly efficient and extraordinarily cheap.

① Container cargo ship.
② Crane.
③ Container fork lift.
④ Container trucks.
⑤ Loading zone.
⑥ Container freight cars.

serving the international market.

Industry's flight had little effect on Lebek's most ancient and revered enterprise: maritime trade. Renovations to the port ensured that it remained one of Northern Europe's most modern and efficient shipping destinations. Europe, meanwhile, had nearly completed the economic integration of its sovereign nations in the European Economic Community. This supranational entity represented enormous economic power and raised still further the commercial prospects for Lebek's port.

Ships from every continent and country chose Lebek as their European port of entry. The city offered arriving container cargo ships well-organized piers, excellent services, affordable fees, and an efficient network of railroads and highways.

Enormous storage tanks were built for the crude oil shipped in by supertankers. Adequate petroleum stores were essential to the functioning of national economies and individual households. New freight platforms and wharves enlarged the already extensive port area, whose growth continued steadily seaward.

Land reclamation projects also continued. Engineers applied the most advanced materials and technologies to the creation of huge dikes capable of withstanding the most powerful storms and flood tides. Ecological concerns were addressed through the construction of sluiceways designed to preserve natural wetlands within the reclaimed parcels.

As the twentieth century drew to a close, Lebek, the city built on the seas, was extending its influence beyond them.

Dikes

Large new dikes were built to provide greater protection to the coast and reclaimed lowlands. The new structures linked points of land with manmade islands to create a barrier chain. Large sluiceways permitted seawater to flow through the barrier, providing the waters behind it with the salinity necessary to support the mollusks and other marine life of the natural ecosystem. In the event of storms, the sluiceways were closed to prevent flooding.

The dikes were built on a foundation of compacted sand, topped with polyurethane, additional sand, gravel, stone, and wire mesh. Concrete pylons were positioned, and stone slabs were used to reinforce the dike base.

① Compacting of undersea land.
② Laying of foundation materials.
③ Positioning of pylons.
④ Raising of pylons.
⑤ Reinforcement of dike base.
⑥ Pylons.
⑦ Sluiceway and gates.

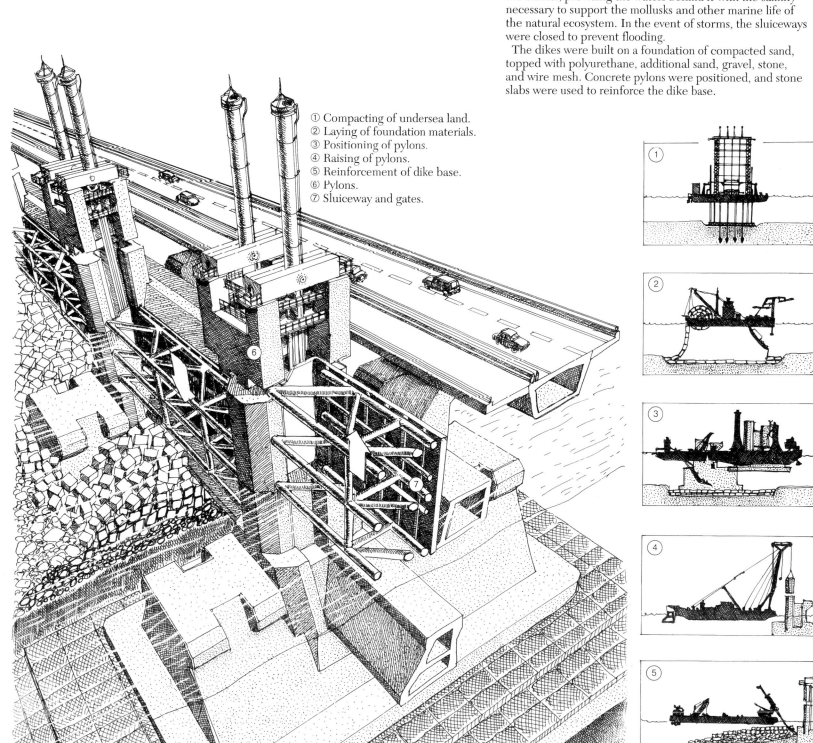

INDEX

1. Settlements and Standing Stones: 1000 B.C.
2. "Dragons" from the North: Late Eighth Century A.D.
3. Free City in Feudal Europe: Early Thirteenth Century
4. The City Built upon Herring: Mid-Fourteenth Century
5. A Mercantile City in Decline: Early Sixteenth Century
6. Water: Ally and Enemy: Early Seventeenth Century
7. Modern Expansion: Mid-Seventeenth Century
8. A Fortified Port: Mid-Eighteenth Century
9. The Slow Transition: Early Nineteenth Century
10. Bursts of Steam: Mid-Nineteenth Century
11. A Major Port Expands: Early Twentieth Century
12. War and a New Beginning: 1940s
13. Megalopolis: 1960s
14. Looking Seaward, Again: Late Twentieth Century